Jewish Latin America
Ilan Stavans, series editor

the book of memories

Translated by Dick Gerdes

Introduction by Ilan Stavans

University of New Mexico Press   Albuquerque

the
book
of
memories

Ana María Shua

Library of Congress Cataloging-in-Publication Data

Shua, Ana María, 1951–
    [Libro de los recuerdos.   English]
    The book of memories / Ana María Shua ; translated by Dick Gerdes;
    introduction by Ilan Stavans.
        p.   cm. — (Jewish Latin America)
    ISBN 0-8263-1948-3 (cloth). — ISBN 0-8263-1949-1 (pbk.)
    1. Gerdes, Dick.   II. Title.   III. Series.
    PQ7798.29.H8L5313   1998
    863—dc21   98–24321
                                                                    CIP

The Book of Memories *is the third volume in the University of New Mexico Press
series* Jewish Latin America. *The Spanish original was completed thanks to a generous grant from the John Simon Guggenheim Memorial Foundation.*

Contents

Introduction

Ilan Stavans

History might not be a Jewish invention, but memory surely is and so is forgetfulness. To remember is to be selective with the past, to forget what is judged unnecessary. Jews are by nature retellers: their existence is testified by the act of remembrance of events protagonized by God, and that act links them to the generations that come before and after. The recollections Jews invoke are beyond history, for History, as Thucydides foresaw centuries ago, ought to be systematic, carefully interwoven—in a word, scientific. But Judaism, in spite of Leopold Zunz's *Wissenschaft des Judentums* ("scriptural exegesis and talmudic legalism ought to be treated with rigor," Zunz once said), is anything but scientific: events are not recalled with precision by using historiographic instruments; neither are they approached as quantifiable data to be placed in a specific space and time. Instead, these events unfold in a mythological sphere, embellished by a multitude of voices past and present that retell them again and again, always adding a twist, an anecdote, a side effect.

If History, with a capital H, is the brainchild of Greek civilization, memory—a memory not only cerebral but emerging from the heart—is a rabbinical creation, the product of what has come to be known as the exilic, postbiblical age. After the destruction of the Second Temple, the homelessness of the Jews has pushed them to turn the matters of memory into a homeland, and they are commanded to cherish them with all their heart. "You shall love your God with all your heart, with all your soul and with all your might," the "Va-a-hafta" announces in the Siddur. Love is thus synonymous with remembrance: "Let these matters, which I command you today, be upon your heart. Teach them thoroughly to your children and speak of them while you sit in your home, while you walk on the way, when you retire and when you arise. Bind them as a sign upon your arm and between your eyes. And write them on the doorsteps of your house and upon your gates."

This maxim—remembrance as a command, remembrance as a homeland—is beautifully conveyed in *The Book of Memories*, a novel by Ana María Shua about anamnesis in Argentina, a nation, it is no secret, where memory in and of itself is a most tarnished institution. Novels are not inherently Jewish or Christian or Muslim; their authors are. But the temptation to call this one "a Jewish book" is too big, if anything because of the way its plot is delivered. At its heart are the Rimetkas, a clan not unlike Shua's own: Yiddish-speaking immigrants from Eastern Europe whose fortune in the New World, their rebellions, their mental illness, their miscegenation and illicit affairs, their advancement and setbacks present a distropian picture of Argentina. The country, Shua assures us, is not the ethnic monolith we have been taught to recognize, made by descendants of Iberians and Italians living side by side with the "blackened" population (the so-called *cabecitas negras*), with Catholicism at their core, filled with whores and corrupt politicians. Instead, it is a religiously diverse, racially promiscuous habitat where Jews happen to have arrived accidentally and accidentally too is how they rule their lives.

Grandfather Gedalia, the Rimetka patriarch, an astute moneylender married to Granny, is a center of gravity in the Old House, the family headquarters in Buenos Aires. But for as much as he is loved and repudiated by his entourage, his private life and inner motives remain a mystery to his successors. One by one, his children—Silvester, Clara, Judith, and Pucho (his daughter Gloria dies an early death of diphtheria)—abandon Yiddish to embrace Spanish. In doing so, they *apparently* take root on native Argentine soil, building a genealogy filled with Trotskyites, psychologists, stingy businessmen, and fortune-tellers: Silvester marries Fortunée, alias The Dumb Turk; Clara is wedded to Yaco, Judith to Ramón, and Pucho to Marita . . . and each is blessed and cursed with more descendants. But appearances are mischievous: the roots never solidify and by the end the reader is fully aware of how complex and ambivalent—not to say lightweight— is the Rimetka's love for Argentina. Their last name was concocted by an immigration official when Grandfather Gedalia first entered the country (he in fact wanted to settle in the true Promised Land: America), but the memory of the entire clan has a similar prefabricated taste: they are baffled and disoriented, navigating without an overall goal.

Such disjointed characters are typical of Jewish fiction in Latin America, but *The Book of Memories* is unique in the way it pays tribute to a recognizable device in Jewish letters—more specifically, in Yiddish literature: the unfolding of the story while two guys talk. Indeed, novels like *Fishke the Lame* by Mendele Mokher Sforim and *Teyve the Dairyman* by Sholem Aleichem, as well as stories like "My Quarrel with Hersh Rasseyner" by Chaim Grade and "The Cafeteria" by Isaac Bashevis Singer, to name only a few, are built by having unlikely interlocutors in dialogue. This device opens all sorts of possibilities:

Jewish life is approached as a debate, a clash of opinions, an encounter. Fiction in the Hispanic world seldom takes this route; it is too concerned with exposing the baroque contradictions in the environment, too obsessed with inner monologues of isolated, unstable creatures. Shua's novel is an exception, though. Its plot unfolds willy-nilly as a couple of anonymous descendants in the clan—granddaughters? distant relatives? perhaps even the Rimetka brothers and sisters themselves?—browse through the old family book known, predictably, as The Book of Memories.

And what sort of book is this? An ethereal item: malleable, intangible, ghostlike, in contrast to *The Book of Memories* the reader holds in hand. A book within a book, a tale within a tale. The strategy is surely as ancient as Scheherazade and *Don Quixote*. (I myself played upon it in my novella *Talia in Heaven*.) But Shua adapts it so as to reflect on the limitations of History and the power of memory. The anonymous voices whose inquisitiveness allows the plot to unravel are puzzled by how selective The Book of Memories is: it never delves into the emotional realm of its characters; nor does it place them in actual history. And sure enough, the whole Rimetka odyssey is mapped out in ahistorical terms. In what year precisely did Grandfather Gedalia arrive in Argentina? When does the rest of the action take place? This is not to say that the novel is free of actual references. Mention is made, for instance, of President Hipólito Yrigoyen, after whom one of Grandfather Rimetka's scions is partially named; and Juan Domingo Perón, a ubiquitous specter in the country from 1945 to 1984 (the Rimetkas call him, in Spanish, *el diablo coludo*), keeps on resurfacing. In fact, the love and hatred for Perón become a family sport of sorts, and thus a leitmotif in their aggregated journey: Grandfather Gedalia's four children are all anti-Peronists; Aunt Judith and her husband even participate in 1955 in the Revolución Libertadora, a coup d'etat that brings about Perón's "second coming," as his return to power is commonly known. In contrast, the next Rimetka generation, in its left-wing pose, not only endorses Peronism but embraces militancy during the *época del miedo*, that is, the dictatorship of 1976–83. And yet, all these references are camouflaged and any attempt at concreteness is deliberately evaded, as if the Rimetkas were fugitives of history, inhabitants of a time outside Time. The resulting feeling is one of dislocation: the Rimetkas tell us less about the country they are part of than about diasporic Jewish existence: they live in limbo, loving and mating in a place called Anywhere. What we know about them is what the family—collectively—has chosen to remember. And that amounts to pure myth.

Myth . . . a genealogy of myth. Ana María Shua is a veteran in the art of retelling. In her novels, stories, children books, cookbooks, and anthologies of Jewish humor, she is adept at rewriting biblical, talmudic, and folkloric tales. She reappropriates Jewish tradition by recycling it, retelling the tale of the Golem of Prague, Hershel Ostropolier, or the wise men of Chelm in a style of her own. And *The Book of Memories*, originally published in 1994, is a vintage example in this art of reiterating by reinterpreting. It illustrates the famous epigraph by French philosopher Emmanuel Levinas: "The Jews are strangers to history. Their world is an abstraction."

the book of memories

Why are you laughing so hard?
Haven't you ever seen a bare ass before?

my grandmother Ana

Almost Like America

Grandfather was skinny when he crossed the ocean. He was real skinny and young, too, and he wasn't a grandfather before leaving Tomachevo to cross the ocean. Grandfather didn't want to come. No one wanted to come here. This wasn't exactly America. It was a poor runner-up. It was dangerous for women. They were put to work as whores. But Granny wasn't a whore, she worked as a seamstress. Back then, men here wore large white scarves that were embroidered.

"You mean handkerchiefs that you put in your pocket? Embroidered handkerchiefs for blowing your nose?"

"Large handkerchiefs like the ones you wear around your neck. White scarves, they said. Can't you hear?"

Grandfather was never persecuted. Grandfather wanted to build America, but not this America, the other one, you know, the real one, the one up north. He was a tailor's apprentice and he was always well dressed. He'd wear those Russian smocks buttoned at the neck and the baggy pants buttoned down at the ankle (like the Cossacks wear in the Russian ballets), made of thick, well-tailored cloth.

And that's the way you'd find Grandfather dressed in Poland, where it was always cold and where everyone ate potatoes. But he was also a deserter. Potatoes on Monday, potatoes on Tuesday, potatoes on Wednesday, potatoes on Thursday, potatoes on Friday, and on Saturdays . . . ah!, that was something different! Saturdays! On Saturdays, fried eggs and potatoes. One would think that Grandfather would've hated potatoes and, with all that meat in America, he'd never have to eat potatoes again. But potatoes are what he liked best. On Saturdays, fried eggs and potatoes.

"Which army did Grandfather desert from?"
"Who knows? Poland was full of armies. There was the Czar's army, the Red Army, the Polish Army, the Polish National Guard. And the Poles supported the Red army and the German army. They all came and went and fought among themselves."

Then one day Grandfather was drafted. It was wartime. Grandfather didn't want to go to war, he wanted to go to America. His fiancée didn't want him to go either, she wanted him to marry her. So he deserted and hid in her house. He hid there for a year, right in her bedroom. And in her bed, too? Grandfather did that? What was he waiting for? He was waiting for the right document. He waited for anyone who got sick, or who might have an accident and die. He was always wearing his nice suit, hiding in his fiancée's house, and waiting for someone to die young so he could buy his identity papers, a nifty legal document belonging to someone who hadn't deserted.

"And what was his fiancée's house like on the outside?"

"It was a house just like any other house."

"And what was his fiancée's house like on the inside?"

"There's a picture of it in The Book of Memories. There's a rug on the ground, and on the rug there's a table, and on the table there's a sewing machine, and around the table there are some chairs, and behind them there's a large piece of furniture made of dark wood, maybe an armoire. And to one side of the table there's a rocking chair and on the other side an armchair."

"Are there pictures on the walls?"

"There weren't any pictures because there were no walls. And around the rug, everything was white, pure white, because it was sitting on the snow. And that's the way his fiancée's house was on the inside. There wasn't enough light inside to take a picture, so they took everything outside and put it in the snow."

Gedalia Rimetka died fairly young and he had a moustache. Grandfather took his identity papers to the American consulate, the real one, the one up north, but they turned him down. Gedalia hadn't died young enough; he just wasn't young enough to be my grandfather. It was always cold in Poland, and it was always snowing. When the snow melted, everything turned to mud. Even the mud was cold.

Grandfather crossed through the mud in Tomachevo, but he really wanted to cross the ocean. So he went to the consulate of this poor America where, he was told, they didn't pay much attention, they didn't understand anything, it was all the same to them. That's America too, but not quite. What's important is to leave Europe, to be able to cross the ocean. Then it'll be easy to get from one America to the other America.

They didn't pay much attention, or they didn't care, or they didn't understand anything, and so Grandfather got ready to cross the ocean. Grandfather Gedalia Rimetka—always elegantly dressed but a little too skinny—boarded the ship in Odessa and started the crossing. They ate the skins of the potatoes, too. Potatoes, however, are full of carbohydrates. Why, then, was Grandfather so skinny? Because he only ate potatoes, and only a few at that.

"Are you sure it was Odessa? Immigrants didn't leave from Odessa? Check The Book of Memories, what does it say?"

"The Book of Memories says that when Grandfather Gedalia boarded ship he was seventeen years old and wore a short-brimmed hat."

The ocean was wide, the ship was Italian. The men slept together in the hold. Was it called the bilge? Grandfather Gedalia didn't know the word *bilge*. Everyone but he vomited everywhere. Gedalia, who was tall and skinny, watched his ship brothers vomit. There were Polish and Russian travelers, and Italians who had gotten on in Genoa. They ate a lot of pasta on board the ship. Lots of macaroni and potato dumplings, but no ravioli. Round pasta, flat pasta, Bologna-style fettuccine with meat sauce, or pesto. That's why by the time Grandfather reached America he wasn't skinny anymore. He gained forty pounds in twenty days. Grandfather ate a lot of pasta but he never got sick. After they reached Brazil, he also ate a lot of bananas.

They arrived first to Pernambuco, where there were lots of blacks and Indians, and it was hot. Grandfather didn't like it there. "This is America?" his fellow travelers asked. They felt deceived. Give up that mud for this mud? Doesn't look promising. Hot mud in America instead of cold mud in Poland? And so they loaded up with bananas. At first they were green, then they turned yellow. Large bunches of mysterious bananas. And that's how a young, skinny, adventurous kid left Odessa and how a dour and fat Grandfather Gedalia arrived in Buenos Aires. He always refused to eat strawberries. They're everywhere in the forests. Bananas are another matter.

"And those on the ship who ate according to the Jewish religion, what did they eat?"

"Those on the ship who ate according to the Jewish religion didn't eat."

And, finally, they arrived. Buenos Aires was a much more acceptable America. It was comparable to Warsaw. It was a real city. He stayed at a hotel for immigrants. Friends were waiting for him. It was cold, not as bad as Poland, but a lot colder than it is now. The cold that the immigrants felt was another type of cold. They would stuff newspapers inside their clothes to stay warm. Newspapers kept you warm, like this, underneath your shirt, yep, whole newspapers.

He lived for a short time in Entre Rios, where the Jewish communities had been established. It was cold there too, especially in the mornings. His fingers would get stiff, numb from the cold, as he milked the cows. Yes, Grandfather wasn't elegant anymore. Grandfather Gedalia was good at making suits, he knew how to cut cloth and sew, but he didn't know how to milk cows or harvest flax. On the other hand, he knew how to ride a horse. And he quickly learned how to eat barbecued meat.

Afterward he went to the city. Then he sent for Granny who had been waiting for him in Tomachevo and he didn't put her to work as a whore but as a seamstress. Then he earned a lot of money. Then he collapsed and died.

"What do you mean, collapsed? Didn't Grandfather Gedalia survive that collapse? Applying hot and cold presses?"

"Grandfather Gedalia survived one collapse but died from another. That's life for you."

Grandfather, said Aunt Judith, was a son of a bitch and he shit all over us. Uncle Pucho said Aunt Judith was a liar and had a dirty mouth. Uncle Pucho never did like women with dirty mouths.

The Name Rimetka

The original Gedalia, the one who died in Poland, the one whose identity papers Grandfather purchased, the one who had died fairly young so that Grandfather's face would coincide with the one in the picture, but not sufficiently young enough to convince the consulate authorities of the real America, the one up north, well, that Gedalia was never called Rimetka exactly.

The surname Rimetka was the result of a combination of auditory expertise and orthographic arbitrariness of some civil servant who attempted to decipher a document written in another language by providing his own interpretation of a surname that he thought a foreigner from Poland should have, which occurred at the time he was taking down Grandfather Gedalia's personal information for the purpose of making his Argentine identification card.

Like so many other immigrants, the Rimetka family had acquired an intensely national name, a truly indigenous product, much more authentically Argentine than a correctly spelled Spanish surname, because Rimetka never existed in Grandfather's homeland, or in the original language or, for that matter, in any other country or time in history.

About Grandfather
Gedalia's Personality

Grandfather Gedalia never wavered in his habits. Every day at five o'clock in the afternoon he would have a cup of English tea at the Richmond Cafe on Florida Street, where he would sit with his friends and watch the women go by.

Not once did he ever set foot in the Richmond on Florida Street. He always went to the Lion Bar instead.

It's possible that Grandfather never set foot in the Richmond on Florida Street (to set foot inside, in the strictest sense of the word) because he always sat at a table on the sidewalk outside. Perhaps he might have set foot inside the premises because he had to go to the bathroom. You might think he would have sat inside when it rained, but that's not true either. He simply didn't go there when it rained because the women wouldn't be out walking.

Grandfather Gedalia would go to the Richmond Cafe and the Lion Bar because he was a moneylender and he had clients at both places.

He would meet his Jewish clients at the Lion Bar and the others at the Richmond Cafe.

Grandfather Gedalia never charged interest on loans to Jewish people because it simply didn't look right. But he also never loaned anything to anyone without charging interest.

They never let moneylenders frequent the Lion Bar.

That's not true.

After he got older, Grandfather Gedalia would meet with his clients in the Pumpernickel, a snack bar that sold hamburgers. Grandfather Gedalia didn't like hamburgers, but he liked The Pumpernickel, mainly because they didn't have waiters and he could spend as long as he liked there without having to buy anything.

Pumpernickel almost rhymes with *kuentenik*. *Kuentenik* means something like moneylender.

Kuentenik doesn't have anything to do with the word moneylender.

Kuentenik is a type of peddler.

In addition to being a moneylender, Grandfather Gedalia was also a *kuentenik*. But he earned more money as a moneylender. As a *kuentenik* he had to do his work on a bicycle until he could afford to buy his first car.

Let's say Grandfather Gedalia would meet with other men in a bar or a coffee shop. They were probably his clients because Grandfather Gedalia never had any friends. There is no doubt that he would watch the women go by. Is everything right so far? Do you agree with what we've said?

No. Grandfather Gedalia was quite charming. He had lots of friends. Most of his friends were immigrants, like him, but he also had some Argentine friends. He was especially proud of them. Not every immigrant had those types of friends.

Many years later, when Grandfather Gedalia would meet someone who was a son of an immigrant he would immediately ask his name and then go on to say that when he was coming over on the ship he had met someone by that same name. Whoever talked to him for the first time found him to be quite charming and would begin questioning him at length about this person he had met in order to see if he or she was part of their family.

Grandfather Gedalia was always terribly stingy.

Grandfather Gedalia was not always terribly stingy.

When Grandfather Gedalia was young, he was very ostentatious. Only after the Crash did he become an Uncle Scrooge.

Grandfather Gedalia became a miser after his children had grown up.

When Grandfather Gedalia bought the Old House he was a real miser about some things, but in others he liked to flaunt his wealth.

Grandfather Gedalia had an Hispanic-Swiss automobile and he would take us out for rides in it. And he had a winter coat of beaver skin made for me and we would vacation in Uruguay. In Pocitos. And if you don't believe me, there are pictures to prove it.

It wasn't Hispanic-Swiss, it was a Packard coupe and we called it "the Packard." We always spent vacations in Mar del Plata. And if you don't believe me, there are pictures to prove it.

If you can't see the statues of those seals, you won't be able to tell if it's Mar del Plata.

You can't tell if it's Pocitos either.

Grandfather Gedalia was an admirer of the Kaiser and that's why he gave Uncle Pucho the name of Isaac Guillermo. He also admired the Germans in general until, that is, the Second World War.

After the Second World War he hated and feared the Germans but he still continued to admire them.

Grandfather Gedalia was for Yrigoyen and that's why he named Uncle Silvester Hipólito, after Hipólito Yrigoyen, who was president of Argentina from 1916 to 1922, reelected in 1928, and deposed in 1930. He originally named him Shloime but the civil servant didn't understand, or he acted like he didn't understand.

Grandfather Gedalia wasn't interested in politics.

In Poland, Grandfather Gedalia was a Communist. After he got to Argentina, he became a materialist.

How was he going to be a Communist and still follow the dictates of his religion? After you become a Communist, there's no going back to your religion.

After that he just stopped being religious. But he followed tradition. Mainly to keep up appearances.

If so, then, why did he throw Aunt Judith out of the house?

Aunt Judith always annoyed everyone, she was unbearable, she was foul-mouthed, so Grandfather Gedalia gave her the boot using her disrespect for our religion as an excuse. In reality, he was the one who wasn't religious.

That's a lie.

What's a lie? If he didn't give a hoot about religion or politics, why did he give Uncle Pucho a name like Hipólito? Because he didn't care one bit about politics. But he was for Yrigoyen just the same.

When Granny would say something, Grandfather Gedalia would always add: she has a big mouth and so she talks. Other times he would say: there is a saying in the Talmud that goes something like this: when people are born stupid, they'll be that way all their lives and the more they talk the more you can tell how stupid they are. Then he would repeat the saying in Hebrew.

Aunt Clara's grandchildren went to a school that taught Hebrew. After that, whenever he would quote the Talmud, he wouldn't repeat it in Hebrew anymore.

Grandfather Gedalia and Granny loved each other very much.

Grandfather Gedalia and Granny had their own special way of loving each other very much.

When Grandfather Gedalia was hiding in Granny's parents' house in order to escape from the Polish army, he never said "she has a big mouth and so she talks too much."

Whenever Grandfather Gedalia didn't like her food, he would throw it on the floor, say, for instance, when there wasn't enough salt or it wasn't hot enough.

When Grandfather Gedalia would be talking and Granny interrupted him, his eyes would well up with tears and he'd look at her as if to say "now that I'm finally old and decrepit doesn't anyone show respect anymore?" When Granny would be talking, Grandfather Gedalia interrupted her all the time.

Grandfather Gedalia sold things on credit.

What kind of things?

Anything. It didn't matter what it was, he just had to sell it on credit.

Is that what it means to be a peddler?

Yes.

At first he peddled his wares on the street, then he went around on a bicycle. But when he got his first car he didn't use it for work, only to take rides.

Grandfather Gedalia used to say that after riding his bike around all morning, a working man had a right to ask his wife to put salt on his food. This meant that if the food didn't have enough salt, a working man had the right to throw it on the floor.

When Grandfather Gedalia got very old, he couldn't eat salt because it was bad for his blood pressure. But he continued to eat hot food.

Selling things on credit was a peddler's life. All the peddlers belonged to a peddlers' co-op. The wives of the peddlers would take things from the co-op and pay for them at cost. But they never bought anything on credit.

Whenever Grandfather Gedalia would tell a lie, he'd pat his left knee.

Grandfather Gedalia suffered from arthritis in his left knee, which had become swollen and deformed, so he'd pat it all day long.

Grandfather had a business selling cloth in La Boca district. Back then, the cloth stores sold more than just silk, even though there were stores that sold fine yard goods.

Whenever the rainy southeast winds would hit La Boca, everything would become flooded, so Grandfather Gedalia would have his Great Inundation Sales.

He would always put his bolts of cloth high up on the shelves so they wouldn't get wet.

In order to sell the cloth at his Great Inundation Sales, he'd wet them down with a bucket of water from the back of the store.

Was he in business in La Boca before or after?

It was after Grandfather Gedalia quit as a peddler but before he became a moneylender.

Grandfather Gedalia was always a moneylender, even in Poland.

Grandfather Gedalia couldn't have been a moneylender in Poland because when he came over he was still very young.

There are people who charge interest while they're still in their mothers' wombs. There are people who, as they're being born, make mortgage loans to the midwives.

Moneylender is just an elegant way of saying loan shark.

There is nothing elegant about being a moneylender.

Grandfather Gedalia was a loan shark and a moneylender. And ever since he quit making his own clothes, he was anything but elegant.

Grandfather Gedalia favored Uncle Silvester because he always got up early and they'd play dominos together.

Uncle Silvester was the only one of Grandfather Gedalia's sons with whom he preferred to talk; for instance, he would go into Silvester's bedroom, look at all of his books, and then ask him how much they'd fetch at the flea market.

I've also heard that one Sunday afternoon he took Silvester on the trolley and then bought him a ham sandwich.

Grandfather Gedalia never ate pig's meat because it was against his religion.

Grandfather Gedalia never ate pig's meat in public.

Grandfather Gedalia was a pig.

The Language

When the eldest of Grandfather Gedalia and Granny's children began attending school, he still hadn't mastered the language of the country (as was customary with the eldest in families of poor immigrants).

This disadvantage, in terms of his relationship with other school mates, caused him great suffering. Yet it didn't take him long to acquire an ample vocabulary equal to the other students, and he quickly learned how to mitigate his syntactical and grammatical errors in Spanish. Nevertheless, it took him years to learn to roll that terrible Spanish double rr, that sonorous alveolar fricative in which the tip of his tongue refused to vibrate like the sound of a motor—you know, vrrrrrrrm—that he would hear other children younger than him pronounce, making him envious, a sound that he could imitate with his upper lip but not with that damned tip of his tongue.

Pucho, the second in line, who learned to speak by imitating Silvester (he imitated everything Silvester did), never did learn how to pronounce that double rr sound either, the same one that Silvester only managed to acquire much later in life, when he was already a teenager.

"Say rrrrregalo," the other children would tell him. Or they'd tell him to say "rr and rr, guitarra" or "rápido ruedan las ruedas, las ruedas del ferrocarril." And when he would write, Silvester always put teritorio for territorio, which surprised his teacher because Silvester was such a good student, so brilliant, a real standard-bearer.

Then, one day, Silvester, who had become visibly upset, arrived at the Old House having made up his mind that never again in that house was anyone going to speak the Other Language, the one his parents had brought over from the Old World: the language that was dying and wasn't even the main language spoken by the majority of people in his parents' native land, or taught in the public schools they had attended. It had been the language commonly used by their parents, among their friends, for children's games and lullabies, for their first words of love, for insulting, and, always, for counting: the only language in which they could do their adding and subtracting. It was that Other Language, the intimate language, the one they could call their own, the true language, the only language, the language that knew no national boundaries, the one language that people joked about, the one so many people called jargon, the language that no one, except for them and others like them, loved and respected. The language was condemned to die with them.

And yet, no one was surprised when Silvester came home from school that day and, even before taking off his school uniform, announced that the teacher had told them to speak only Spanish at home.

Grandfather Gedalia liked the idea for two reasons: it enhanced his work as a peddler, that is to say, as a salesman, because it was a good opportunity to improve his own Spanish. And also because it gave him the opportunity to humiliate his wife in front of his children (which gave him much pleasure).

For Granny, who didn't even manage well in the language of the majority in her own country back home, Spanish seemed like a harsh, unexpressive language that was, above all, inaccessible. Up until that time, she had done her shopping mainly by gesturing and smiling. That was when the butcher at the meat market would give her liver for the cat. Granny would point at the bloody piece of meat and smile embarrassingly while the butcher wrapped it up in a large piece of newspaper.

But if that's what the teacher had ordered, that's the way it had to be. Granny was a little afraid of the teacher who to her seemed more like a member of the border patrol under orders from the immigration authorities keeping an eye on immigrant families and making sure they conform, integrate, and become lost in the big melting pot.

And, hence, that's how the grandparents became identified with the language of lullabies, love, and insults that in time began to disappear, at least on the surface of things, from the home of the Rimetka family. Once it became confined to the master bedroom, the two younger children, Pucho and Clara, never did fully grasp the language.

Beyond the bedroom, Grandfather Gedalia was quite happy not understanding his wife in Spanish, just as they didn't understand each other in their native language. For that reason, you will only find Spanish in The Book of Memories.

A Game of Soccer
(193?) in the Back Yard
of the Old House

It's hard to imagine Uncle Silvester making Uncle Pucho eat soap.

Uncle Silvester was always a man of principles.

As proof, there's the story about the time when that small socialist clandestine press was raided by the police. Uncle Silvester was under age and a Trotskyite, but he was a man of principles. Since he wasn't present at the time, he went down to the police station and turned himself in, claiming to be an accomplice to the criminal acts of writing, printing, and distributing clandestine material in opposition to the government of the Long-tailed Devil (which is what the poor little Crazy-Lady-Around-the-Corner called Perón in her mystical deliriums). The police chief tried to convince him to go home, but it's not easy to persuade a man of principle, especially when he's young, that is, really young.

That's why it's so hard to imagine Uncle Silvester making Uncle

Pucho eat soap. And yet it says in The Book of Memories that when Pucho refused to play soccer, Silvester would make him eat soap.

Probably in the name of one of his principles but, unfortunately, none were ever written down.

Uncle Pucho didn't like playing soccer because he was no good at it, mainly because he always got out of breath—he had asthma—and because in the back yard of the Old House they always played rough and he didn't like getting his shins kicked all the time.

If Aunt Judith had ever said she didn't want to play soccer, he would have made her eat soap too, but she always wanted to play.

None of the nieces and nephews ever met Aunt Gloria. She couldn't play soccer either because she had already nearly died from diphtheria—when she was small.

Aunt Clara never played because she was always trying to act prim and proper.

Aunt Judith wasn't very proper, and she always scored goals with that awesome left kick of hers. On the other hand, in her sewing classes that Granny sent her to, where she could learn something useful in life, her buttonholes would turn out very uneven because they would make her sew with her right hand. In reality, knowing how to sew buttonholes didn't help Aunt Judith at all in life and, for that matter, neither did her dazzling ability to play center forward.

If he had to choose between playing soccer or eating soap, Uncle Pucho always chose soccer. Apparently, only one time did Uncle Silvester actually manage to stick soap into Pucho's mouth. He just pretended to swallow it and then spit it out when his brother wasn't looking. The only thing mentioned in The Book of Memories is that the soap was blue. Since Pucho couldn't run much, they made him goalie.

There were two places to play soccer in the Old House. One was in the Vestibule. Playing soccer in the Vestibule was not allowed.

When Grandfather Gedalia still liked to show off his wealth, there were large vases from some ancient dynasty, porcelain plates that looked like they were from France, little Art Nouveau statues of nude women that were strictly artistic, that is, visibly asexual, and the remains of some vaguely Japanese dishware, neatly arranged in a glass china cabinet.

They played soccer in the Vestibule only at certain times, for instance, when it rained or when Granny was taking her nap or she had gone to her bedroom with her servant Blanca Argentina to listen to the radio, with the kettle boiling next to her and drinking her maté tea. Of course, they also played there when Grandfather wasn't at home. But as soon as they would hear his footsteps on the stairs—and sometimes it wasn't soon enough—Silvester, Pucho, and Judith would scurry away with their friends to hide under their beds.

Whenever they would play soccer in the Vestibule, they tempered their soccer moves by playing with intelligence and precision, where control replaced strength, and something would always get broken.

They could play better out back, where there was a guayaba tree, a crab apple tree, a twisted pomegranate tree, vines in the corners, and grass. When Grandfather still liked to show off, the grass was meticulously groomed by a gardener who came every fifteen days. When Grandfather turned into a miser, the yard turned to weeds. The famous game that is the topic of this chapter took place when he still liked to show off. There was a large, open space at the back where they could play a great game of soccer. Before the First World War, no one played soccer in the small villages in Poland. However, Grandfather Gedalia never prevented Silvester and his friend Pedro from spending an entire weekend building goal posts out of some sticks.

Looking straight to the back—one could watch from the second-story veranda overlooking the courtyard—there were two lemon trees and a palm tree. The palm tree was tall, wide, produced small co-

conuts, and was smack dab in the middle of the soccer field. All the kids from the surrounding neighborhood could dodge that tree with their eyes closed, but the Rimetka brothers could also use it to their advantage (as a part of their defense).

Playing on their turf, the ability to dodge the palm tree was, without a doubt, one of the two important advantages the Rimetka Boys team had over the other teams; the other advantage was having Aunt Judith play center forward.

The Rimetka Boys was made up of the Rimetka brothers (Pucho always played goalie), Pedro (Silvester's friend who later became a Trotskyite), and the twin brothers from Down-the-Block). The playing field was perfect for challenging matches of six against six.

The Rimetka Boys were almost unbeatable in the neighborhood. But there was another team of rough kids who were bigger that could always tie them at least, and sometimes even beat them, especially when they played the big matches. They were called the Bacacay Juniors and they liked to call themselves The-Best-Soccer-Team-in-Flores. Pucho was as afraid of the Bacacay Juniors as he was of his brother Silvester.

Written in clumsy sports slang of the soccer world, there makes mention in The Book of Memories of one of those great matches. It's almost useless to try to compare that document with the memories of those who were there and saw what actually happened, either as observers or players. Most of the eyewitness accounts represent a whole gamut of impervious but fond memories in which goals, players, and rivals who were gathered at the Old House became intertwined and confused. Pucho and Judith probably remember that last goal very well but they won't talk about it.

"It was a sad day to have been present at that match between the Rimetka Boys and the Bacacay Juniors. Everyone witnessed one of the ugliest games ever, if it's at all possible to talk about aesthetics in sports. It was probably the worst of the year and here, fans, we're talking about ethics and morals in Argentine soccer."

The fans who went to see that game were mostly the players of other neighborhood teams that were generally made up of those who lived on the same street or were in the same grade at school. They didn't always root for the same team.

The only real fans of the Rimetka Boys were Aunt Clara and Martita, who was a cousin of the twin brothers from Down-the-Block and who had brought a banner tied to two broomsticks that at one point broke and got trampled.

The only fan of the Bacacay Juniors, at least during the first half of the match, was the goalie's younger brother, whose parents said he had to tag along. The number doubled after the first half when the center forward for the Bacacay Juniors, Four-Eyes, broke his glasses and spent the rest of the game squinting from the sidelines.

Near the end of the game, the one-and-only Gedalia Rimetka, appeared at the railing of the patio and watched the game, even though he seemed to be staring off into space, as if he were making complicated mathematical calculations based on compound interest which was, most likely, what was going on in his head.

"Without a doubt this game will be remembered as the worst one of the year. Considering that one of the key players was the champion no less, it was even more serious, since they were playing on home turf."

(Nowadays, Aunt Judith's legs are kind of pale and fat and covered with varicose veins. And her left leg isn't much different from her right one either. However, back then her left leg, her famous goal-kicking leg, was the one preferred by the guys, when Judith was nine years old).

If there was something about which the spectators could unanimously agree, it was their undisputed admiration for Judith, who always received an ovation when she went onto the field. They were all so impressed with how well she played that in the nonchampionship games, they would make her play half the game on each side. But in the championship games, she only played for the Rimetka Boys. And even more this time in which, unfortunately, the honor of the family and the entire block was at stake.

"The visiting team, Bacacay Juniors, began playing at an uncompromisingly slow pace, as if they had lead in their pockets. If they managed, indeed, at some point to throw the Rimetka Boys team into chaos, it wasn't because of their playing merits or to the detriment of the champion player, but rather it was due to the deterioration of the spectacle. When, at the same time, the Rimetka Boys began stalling, everyone in the gallery lost their patience and began whistling and hissing in unison.

Due to the force of the outside forwards, the Rimetka Boys were in control of the offensive for the first thirty minutes. But they didn't need to perform any more than necessary because they were also aided by the lackluster showing of the Bacacay defense. By the end of the first half there was one injury and they were tied at four goals apiece."

But when the Bacacay Juniors' center forward broke the left lens of his glasses, the visiting team refused to continue playing unless Judith went over to play on their side. If it had been a matter of playing by professional rules, their arguments would have been deemed ridiculous. But the Bacacay Juniors was a stubborn group and there wasn't one among them that Uncle Silvester was capable of making eat soap. At that point the majority of the fans seemed clearly in favor of the visiting team, whose reasoning was based on the following:

1. Missing a player in a game where there are six players per team was too much of a disadvantage;
2. In addition, to have Judith playing for her brothers' team meant sure death;
3. The Rimetka Boys were so used to the palm tree that it was like having an extra player;
4. Frankly, Judith who was worth two players and, if you include the palm tree, the Rimetka Boys had eight players while the Bacacay Juniors were down to five players;
5. Therefore, eight against five wasn't fair.

There was no use in trying to tell those little brats that in professional play if you don't have substitutes, you're screwed. And the Rimetka Boys countered by arguing that Judith's offensive capabilities were compensated by the poor showing of their goalie. In effect, Uncle Pucho had been hoping that if he continued to play lousily they would throw him out of the game.

Finally, with a group of fans serving as arbitrators, they came to an agreement: the Rimetka Boys would loan their center forward to the Bacacay Juniors, but only for the last five minutes of the game. They had an alarm clock belonging to Granny that would make sure everything was calculated down to the last second.

And those were the fatal five minutes for the Rimetka Boys. Because when Judith was on the attack, she really attacked, taking repeated shots at the goal, dodging the other team's defense, and scrambling hard to get a goal no matter which team she was on.

"Judith Rimetka is an ace player who always plays fairly. She makes shots at the goal with precision and strength. When she eludes her opponents by handily side-stepping them, everyone always thinks of how well Ludovico Bidoglio used to play. As her confused rivals try to catch up to her, about all that's left is the shining figure of Judith Rimetka with her pursuers forming a comet with a long tail."

It might seem strange that Judith would play with the same enthusiasm for the Bacacay Juniors that she would for her brothers' team. But her enthusiasm was justified: she shared with her brother Silvester an innate sense of ethics; she had to demonstrate at any cost that females were also good goal scorers; and it gave her a perverse pleasure to score goals against her dimwit brother Pucho.

"During that unfortunate game, Judith Rimetka's playing skills were the only thing that gave anyone a little satisfaction. J. R. is perfectly capable of executing that classic play that the old men still talk about, the one where you steal the ball from the opponent from behind, that mythic play of the great Jorge Brown who played on the legendary Alumni team. Basically, while the enemy advances at a fast pace, Judith Rimetka cranks up speed from behind and, calculating the distance she needs to reach them, steps in front of her opponent, maneuvers the ball away from him, and runs to the side, completing a perfect semicircular move called a "half moon." When Judith stops the ball from advancing down field, that means the end of the attack. She has fully demonstrated her ability to play perfectly."

Pucho was afraid of Silvester. He would play badly hoping they would kick him out of the game, but he didn't want to play so badly that they'd accuse him of letting goals in on purpose. In general, Pucho wasn't afraid of Aunt Judith, but when she started playing for the other side, during those last five minutes, then he grew afraid of her. Since it was four to four, and if Judith scored a goal, Silvester would hit him for being a queer and a crummy goalie. Due to Pucho's asthma,

Silvester called him a wheezer and a nobody, he was mommy's favorite, and he was afraid to play football and all those kinds of things.

"The Rimetka Boys' goalie, who had seen the ball enter his net four times that afternoon, was not prepared to defend his goal very well against the center forward for the Bacacay Juniors. A seemingly imperfect shot by Judith flustered the home team goalie: her unanticipated drive forward, which surprised him, caused him to trip over himself. Up until that goal, he had been impaired by being discredited for his lack of skillfulness which, in turn, heightened the moment-by-moment chaotic pulse of the spectacle."

You had to be ready for Judith's left foot and it wasn't the first time that Pucho had intercepted one of her shots. But during that last second, at the moment when the goalie was ready for that demolishing blow, Judith tripped on the bumpy ground—she was wearing Silvester's over-sized shoes—and lost control of the ball. Despite the setback, she managed to kick the ball with her right foot—a seemingly weak shot—which looked deceptively easy, as it rolled along the ground. Then Pucho lunged at it, expecting to intercept it. That was the only thing anyone could have done. No one would have thought that the damn soccer ball, bouncing triumphantly and gleefully over his head, was going to spin off a rock before the unfortunate Rimetka Boys' goalie could grab it, making the home team goalie look pretty bad.

Pucho, sprawled out on the ground and breathing in the dust floating around him, spies a forest of grass, a string of ants carrying away a dead cricket, a solitary coin, and Judith's footprint that looked like a road map stamped into the dirt. He sees how close he was to the ball, with his hands extended, almost touching it and, then, afterward, although he can still see it, he hears, above all he hears the screaming of joy and the screams of anger.

He doesn't get up immediately, so he continues watching an ant carry off part of a palm leaf that's twice his size, then he sees the cricket move a little, seemingly alive as he's pulled along by the hoard of ants, and then he notices that some of the reeds of grass are dark green, others are almost yellow, and still others are juicy, spring green in color. And he thinks about all the ways in which things could have turned out differently: if he could've leaped a little sooner, or a little later, or a little further, and if Judith hadn't tripped, or how her kick could have been different, Judith's famous kick, making the shot more predictable, or how he, for instance, without lunging, could have jumped back a few steps and let the ball nail him in the chest. Or how maybe he shouldn't even have been born.

And, although it's neither the first time nor the last, and while it's not a very important match, and none of the players or the spectators will ever remember it, after so many games, those thousands of games that the Rimetka brothers played in the back yard of the Old House, and its children (with that bland mass of memories in which everything becomes confused—goals, the opposition, fans, and soccer balls), this is the goal that will always haunt him, Aunt Judith with her skinny legs and wearing those enormous soccer shoes, that cricket and the ants, and that unexpected, fatal shot.

Many years later, Uncle Pucho's daughter, The Indian Girl, who had already grown up (her mother, Uncle Pucho's second wife, had already been cut up into pieces, with nothing left of her) and Uncle Pucho were sitting in the dining room of the Old House. She was rubbing his head with a new substance to prevent baldness and Uncle Pucho saw the brown age spots on his hands and thought that even if his hair did grow (he hoped it would but he didn't expect it to), he wouldn't get any younger for it.

And he also thought he was a real nobody, not just a plain nobody, but a downright no-good nobody, and he was disgusted with himself. And it's important to say here that The Indian Girl, who by that time knew she had been adopted, loved him very much and, with that loving animal care, she looked like a young monkey picking lice from her monkey father's head.

Then Pucho began to realize that everything ends up the same (generally, he never thought about anything more than Ferro's performance in the B League championship, and even that wasn't much to think about). Everything ends in death, but when each little thing starts out in life it has a different beginning and he, Pucho, had begun to be a downright no-good nobody the day he couldn't stop that fucking goal his little sister had kicked in. That fucking goal.

Aunt Judith

Aunt Judith said no one helped her down the stairs with the suitcases. By no one she meant none of her fucking brothers or sisters. That's the way she put it.

Her fucking siblings included Aunt Clara, Uncle Silvester, who was the oldest of the family, and Uncle Pucho, who was the youngest brother.

Uncle Pucho said that he personally helped Aunt Judith take her suitcases down the stairs, and he said Uncle Silvester and Josafat, the servant, did the same thing. Aunt Judith said that only Josafat had helped her. In those days, the rich had servants and the Rimetka family was rich.

In The Book of Memories, there's a description of the staircase in the Old House: it was long, wide, and made of marble. It had a landing in the middle separated by a door made of wood with beveled glass. It was always open. The front door, on the first floor which was decorated with black wrought iron, was always locked. After the landing, the second flight of stairs was steeper and the steps were narrower. The shiny, mahogany banister ended right at that dangerous point where you had to stay close to the wall that was also tiled in marble.

That's the way the staircase was. It's still the same, but it doesn't have any memories.

Uncle Pucho met his military obligation by serving as an artillery gunner, and he used to sing a song that began: "The roaring thunder (pause) has already sounded. . . ." Uncle Pucho said that night (the night Aunt Judith left) he was wearing his army uniform and only carried down the brown suitcase, the pigskin one, because he needed one hand free to keep his army cap from falling off his head.

Josafat was coming down with Aunt Judith's black carry-all, when Uncle Silvester sped past him to open the door. And if that's not the way it was, Uncle Pucho would say, then tell me how Aunt Judith managed to open the door downstairs if the only person who had a key was Uncle Silvester, since he was the oldest.

Aunt Clara said she helped too, for she and Aunt Judith had packed the bags together, then they cried, and when the emotion was running high, Clara gave her a pure silk and lace blouse that was beautiful. She regretted it afterward because Judith never wore it, always saying that pure silk made her perspire too much.

Aunt Judith said Aunt Clara had shit for brains and she had neither any proof nor any witnesses to say that she hadn't worn that famous blouse, mainly because they hadn't seen each other in years. She also said Aunt Clara knew perfectly well that pure silk made her, Clara, sweat like a horse and that she had given her the blouse only because she had grown tired of it and because there was a stain of apple juice on the front that wouldn't come out.

While she talked, Aunt Clara used a rag and mineral spirits to polish the cut-glass pendants on the immense chandelier that hung over the dining room table in her apartment on Alvear Avenue. It was the very same one that had hung over the dining room table of the Old House. Aunt Clara's hands were so covered with brown spots it was no use to try to rub them out with the spirits because they wouldn't have gone away no matter what. The chandelier, said Aunt Judith, shouldn't have been in Aunt Clara's house. Whenever Aunt Judith drank coffee, the little cup always shook in her hand. Whenever she drank whiskey, she would get all giggly. But this time, even though she had drank some whiskey, she wasn't happy at all.

Aunt Clara said Aunt Judith had always felt bitter because of the way her husband had treated her, and, even though she didn't know why, as far back as when she was young, even as an adolescent, she always felt resentful, which is why she reminded her of Eva Perón.

Aunt Judith wouldn't have liked to be told that anyone considered her an embittered person; she would have preferred that everyone see her as an independent woman who was ahead of her time. But the worst insult would have been to compare her to the wife of the Long-tailed Devil (Perón), because Judith had been a part of the anti-Peronist forces. Judith and her husband, Uncle Ramón, had transported arms in boxes of the Federal Soap Company in the trunk of their car when they collaborated to overthrow Perón. That must be why Aunt Judith—who didn't believe in God—used to say that the Asshole in the sky—and she'd look up—punished her with a Peronist for a daughter. When the 1955 Revolution of Liberation outlawed the name of The-One-I'm-Referring-To, that is, Perón, the Rimetka family decided to call him what the little Crazy-Lady-Around-the-Corner called him in her mystical deliriums: the Long-tailed Devil.

Nevertheless, Aunt Clara loved her sister Judith very much and whenever they'd run into each other Clara's expression would soften and she would be delighted to see her. Aunt Judith always spoke loudly, drank whiskey, smoked, and did many things that other people wouldn't dare, all of which made Aunt Clara feel afraid, envious, and happy.

Uncle Pucho used to say Aunt Clara had a strong personality like Aunt Judith and that's why they were always at odds. He'd talk about it while meticulously sorting through innumerable tiny boxes of gemstones in his apartment where he had seen so many of his businesses fail, like the time he became a wholesaler for dressmaking notions, which later became known as costume jewelry. Uncle Pucho never had a very strong personality.

To Grandfather Gedalia, that jewelry was pure imitation if it didn't have a strictly functional quality about it. For instance, it smacked of imitation to put marble tiles on the walls of the staircase, or to hang fancy chandeliers with glass pendants, or to have molded plaster baseboards, or to use imitation goblets like they had done in the Old House. When he pronounced the word *imitation,* he hummed the *m* in disapproval to make his message clear.

Uncle Silvester used to say Grandfather Gedalia was intelligent because when he suffered a Collapse and he woke up one day and found Aunt Judith next to his bed, he said good morning as if he had just seen her the day before. Never again did he say a word about her problems. It had been seventeen years since Aunt Judith had descended the staircase of the Old House with the help of Josafat and with or without the help of her brothers and sister.

Aunt Judith never said Grandfather was intelligent. She always called him a rotten son-of-a-bitch and a farting hypocrite whose interest in religion only concerned what the neighbors might say, that is, he was all show and no go.

Uncle Pucho said Aunt Judith was not only a liar but also foul-mouthed. He said it many times on different occasions. Uncle Pucho never liked foul-mouthed women. It must have been because they reminded him of his sister Judith.

Aunt Clara said Aunt Judith tended to exaggerate things but basically she was a good person.

The Book of Memories doesn't say anything about their real characters. On the other hand, where it refers to his Collapse, it says Grandfather Gedalia had an oxygen tent over his bed and oxygen bottles were constantly coming and going down the hallway, rolled along on their round bottoms by the attendants because they were too heavy to carry. A famous doctor came to the house and prescribed ice packs and hot water bottles, and that's how Grandfather recovered from the Collapse.

When Aunt Clara had finished cleaning the chandelier, she started in on the moldings of the china cabinet that Grandfather Gedalia also said was imitation. Aunt Clara would wrap her finger in a yellow flannel dusting cloth and, using the tip, she'd carefully wipe every contour, leaving a small semicircular spot on the cloth that matched her fingernails underneath, as proof that the cleaning had been necessary, which brought great satisfaction to her.

Uncle Pucho said that in addition to being a liar, Aunt Judith was a troublemaker and was always creating discord.

Uncle Silvester used to say that Aunt Judith, when she was young, could play soccer really well, and he would loan her some pants and soccer shoes to wear, and they'd always put her in as center forward. Since Uncle Pucho didn't know how to play at all, they made him goalie because if he ran a lot his asthma would start up.

Aunt Judith married the love of her life: Uncle Ramón. Uncle Ramón was bald and paunchy, smelled funny, and always told dirty jokes. Aunt Judith used to say they had met at a birthday party and, at first, after they were introduced, they spoke very formally to each other. Six months had passed before they first kissed each other on the mouth. Those days are documented in the letters that Uncle Ramón used to send to Aunt Judith via Martita, her best friend, who was a cousin of the twins from Down-the-Block and who, when she was small, was a fan of the Rimetka Boys team.

Uncle Silvester said that Aunt Judith and Uncle Ramón, in their own way, were always very happy together.

Aunt Clara said they were never happy together because Uncle Ramón suffered from a disease: heavy drinking.

Uncle Pucho used to say Uncle Ramón was a total drunk and it wasn't a disease but an outright sin.

Aunt Judith would only say her husband had become an expert in the area of mixed drinks.

The Book of Memories states how Uncle Ramón would do his One-Armed Violinist routine at family get-togethers. In order to have just one arm, he would stick the other inside his shirt and put his jacket over his shoulders. The right sleeve of the jacket and the empty shirt sleeve would hang limp, creating an impressive effect. Tucking an imaginary violin under his chin, he pretended to play it with his left hand, using whatever he had handy as a bow. About halfway through his performance, Uncle Ramón would pretend to drop the bow but then he would catch it with one of his fingers of his hidden hand, which would be sticking out of the fly of his pants. It was a great act and everyone would laugh and applaud, everyone, that is, but Uncle Pucho.

Uncle Pucho always said the One-Armed Violinist act was gross and inappropriate and whenever Uncle Ramón would announce he was going to do it, Uncle Pucho would call to his second wife and his only daughter, The Indian Girl, and they would head for the dining room.

Aunt Judith used to say Uncle Pucho was henpecked and he did exactly what his second wife—that frumpy whore who thought she was pretty high class—told him to do. Everyone agreed that perhaps this observation was a little unfair because before they cut her to pieces it's true Uncle Pucho's second wife was, in effect, very fat, and while it's possible that she acted a certain way, she really wasn't a whore.

After Grandfather's Collapse and Judith returned to the Old House, Uncle Ramón, who was Aunt Judith's husband, began taking part in the family get-togethers. Aunt Clara would say she felt a bit sorry for Aunt Judith because of what she had gone through after marrying a man who, in the end, had made her life so miserable. Aunt Judith said Aunt Clara was envious because she, Aunt Judith, had married for love, whereas Aunt Clara had married out of convenience to a man who was a thousand years older, who was impotent and chased women on the side.

Uncle Silvester used to say Aunt Judith had gone to bed with Uncle Ramón before they got married and she had used him as an alibi so they could go to Tiger Park where people can eat a meal and spend the night. Uncle Silvester started doing well in business after he began working for his father-in-law, The Dumb Turk's father. He was the first one to become independent, leave the Old House, and buy himself a car.

Aunt Judith used to say Uncle Silvester would pervert young girls because he would always take different ones, the younger the better, to that park. But she always said it laughingly, wanting to demonstrate she wasn't scandalized by it because, in effect, she was proud of Silvester: he was her favorite brother.

Aunt Clara had said Aunt Judith, when she tried to commit suicide, had taken a whole bottle of Seconal, a sedative. Uncle Pucho said Aunt Judith had downed an entire container of Folidol, used for killing ants. Some of the pages in The Book of Memories are blank and others have been ripped out.

Aunt Clara used to say that when someone really wants to kill himself, he does it without telling anyone and, in Aunt Judith's case, she had called Martita to tell her that she was taking a whole bottle of a sedative, called Seconal. Aunt Clara talked with authority because her son was a psychologist. But she was also envious, so said Uncle Silvester, because Aunt Judith had called Martita instead of her, Aunt Clara, who was her only sister and who had lived in the same house with her.

Whenever Aunt Clara would talk about Aunt Judith, her husband who was impotent and chased after other women, would leave the room so he wouldn't have to listen.

Aunt Judith said when she took the bottle of Veronal (Seconal didn't exist then), she didn't tell anyone, much less her friend Martita, even though if she had decided to tell someone it would have been her—a woman who had balls—and not her sister Clara who, at the drop of a hat, would shit her pants. And, it was just by chance, said Aunt Judith, that her brother Silvester had found her dying in bed wearing her best party outfit, a long white Chanel-style dress with a short matching jacket.

Uncle Pucho said Martita, Aunt Judith's best friend, had phoned Uncle Silvester and told him his sister had downed a container of Folidol, an ant killer that unlike the strong sedative Veronal could be purchased without a prescription. Uncle Pucho said while Silvester was trying to help Judith, he was the one who called for an ambulance. He also said he had to pay off the ambulance drivers so they wouldn't report it to the police because suicide was against the law. Uncle Pucho used to say whoever commits suicide should be given the death penalty.

Aunt Judith said having to pump out her stomach was much worse than a roller-coaster ride and no one should have to go through it; only a fool would ever commit a second suicide with poison after having gone through that.

Aunt Clara said Aunt Judith, dressed up in a dashing black outfit, was lying on her bed as if asleep and taking her last breaths or something like that.

Uncle Pucho said Aunt Judith never did learn how to dress appropriately because she always wore those gaudy colors.

Uncle Silvester said that when he saw his sister Judith dying in her bed he didn't pay any attention to what she was wearing.

Aunt Judith said Granny had always loved Aunt Clara more than her. She said when she was young her mother didn't love her because she had a snub nose that looked like the rear end of a chicken, and Granny would tap Judith's nose three times with her middle finger and say to her nose, nose, nose, why don't you grow, and that's why it grew so much.

Uncle Pucho used to say Granny was a very affectionate woman and, from the minute Aunt Judith was born, her nose looked like a giant siphon.

Aunt Clara said Granny pampered Uncle Pucho more than anyone else because he had asthma.

Uncle Silvester said Uncle Pucho couldn't remember the day Aunt Judith was born because he was too small. Uncle Pucho said he remembered it very well because he had lugged Aunt Judith's cradle out of his parent's bedroom.

Uncle Silvester used to say Aunt Judith had done the right thing when she took her suitcases down the stairs of the Old House to elope with Uncle Ramón because everyone has a right to live however they want. Uncle Pucho said he personally helped her carry out the pigskin suitcase, which was the heaviest of all, because he was tired of so much arguing and fighting and was delighted that Aunt Judith was leaving once and for all. With his head stuck under the hood of the car, Uncle Pucho was talking as if he were seducing the motor. Uncle Pucho really did talk to those motors, touching and caressing them ever so gently, and getting them to do things no one else could. The motors would just purr away, like a woman who warms up to the man who knows how to arouse her.

Uncle Silvester used to say if Uncle Pucho would have had just a little more confidence in himself and a little more smarts in business, and with that ability he had for mechanics, he could have earned a lot of money, or at least more than he actually earned in reality.

Aunt Judith used to say Uncle Pucho was given to screwing his cars and that's why his second wife was a sourpuss, and there's no need to even mention his first wife, which is why he had to adopt his only daughter.

Aunt Clara insisted Aunt Judith was a resentful person because her husband, whenever he got drunk, would beat her. Aunt Clara was short and chubby and her skin would roll up into rings around her wrists, like a little baby's, which were separated by bracelets.

Aunt Judith, who was neither fat nor skinny, would say Uncle Ramón never got drunk because he knew how to drink. He wasn't like the wimps in her family who would get smashed by just taking a whiff. She also said never once, never ever, did he raise a hand to her.

Aunt Clara said she—Aunt Judith—began to call her on the telephone after she had escaped from the Old House to marry Uncle Ramón. Wearing her robe and stretched out on the bed, that's what she said.

Aunt Judith said Aunt Clara didn't start calling her right away, it took her a long time to begin communicating with her again and all of her brothers and sister treated her like the cow dung they themselves were and didn't pay any attention to her for the longest time, and, if they would run into her on the street, they'd look the other way. She said one time she called her parents' house and when that foolish old Granny heard her voice, she shit her pants and slammed down the receiver. Aunt Judith said she didn't see her mother again until Grandfather suffered a Collapse.

Uncle Pucho said when Aunt Judith had her first child Granny began visiting her without Grandfather Gedalia knowing about it, and she always went home afterward crying over the cruel things Aunt

Judith would say to her. Uncle Pucho always hoped she would swallow her tongue and choke to death like some epileptic.

Aunt Clara used to say if Granny could come back from the grave and see one of her sons working as a mechanic, like Uncle Pucho and, moreover, her one and only Uncle Pucho, her favorite child, she'd jump right back into her own grave.

Uncle Silvester said he thought it was wrong for Aunt Judith to convert and marry in a church. But what was one to do? Aunt Judith said she couldn't care less where she got married—she didn't believe in religion anyway—and the only thing she wanted to do was live with Uncle Ramón, who knew how to make the most of good whiskey and enjoy life.

The Book of Memories states that Uncle Ramón also knew a lot of dirty jokes and he would tell them at every party, right after dinner. And Aunt Judith would invariably break out laughing, but it always seemed a little forced because living with Uncle Ramón she surely knew every joke by heart.

Uncle Pucho said Uncle Ramón converted the family's assets into whiskey and drank it up. That's why Aunt Judith had to move to that tiny apartment where the paint was peeling off the walls and she had no money to give them a new coat. Uncle Pucho also lived in a small apartment where the dirty paint was peeling off the walls and, although he saw the walls every day, he never thought much about it.

Aunt Judith told the story about one day when everyone was sitting at the dining room table and Grandfather stood up and said no daughter of his who was seeing a Gentile was going to eat at his table. Aunt Judith said she had no intention of leaving neither the table nor her boyfriend. So then Grandfather Gedalia, who had never touched her—not even to give her a hug or a kiss, according to Aunt Judith—got up from his chair and grabbed her by the arm and took her into the hall and struck her. And then he threw her down on the floor, according to Aunt Judith, and kicked her until her body turned black and blue and told her, according to Aunt Judith, she wasn't his daughter anymore.

She went to her room and cried and cried and then put on her white Chanel-style dress with the short white waist jacket so she could die in high style, or she got undressed down to her black petticoat, or she just left her normal gaudy clothes on, whichever, and downed an entire bottle of Veronal or Seconal or Folidol . . . the entire bottle.

Uncle Pucho said Grandfather Gedalia was withdrawn and very stern but, so long as money wasn't involved, basically he was a decent person. His bark was worse than his bite, and he never hit anyone, not even Aunt Judith, who was foul-mouthed and for whom a whipping might have done some good. Whenever Uncle Pucho talked about Grandfather Gedalia and didn't mention Aunt Judith and her problems, it never occurred to him to compare him to a decent person.

Aunt Clara says Grandfather Gedalia never hit her, except the time he slapped her in the face for throwing a brick at Aunt Gloria who died when she was little, not from the blow of the brick but from diphtheria.

Uncle Silvester said when Aunt Judith had recuperated from having her stomach pumped, she decided to run away with Uncle Ramón. Her brothers and sister helped her.

Aunt Clara said her son the psychologist explained to her that if a person threatens to commit suicide, he or she is bordering on hysterics and generally hysterical people don't commit suicide on purpose, although one has to be careful in these matters because things can get out of hand and they really do die.

Uncle Pucho said Aunt Judith dated Uncle Ramón for two years before they got married. Uncle Silvester said they were engaged for three. Aunt Judith said they had been going out secretly for four.

Uncle Silvester said Grandfather Gedalia was a master at dominoes. The Book of Memories confirms it.

The Fiber Glass Business

One day, the Devil (the real one, not the other one the Crazy-Lady-Around-the-Corner talked about) appeared before Uncle Silvester. And even though he didn't have a beard or goat's feet or smell of sulphur or have a tail or a trident, he still recognized him all the same because he had Grandfather Gedalia's face and the hands of a history professor who Uncle Silvester remembered from high school. The professor had a round, chubby face but his hands, holding the grade book as he chose a student to recite something, were unforgettable: they were horrible, he had the hands of the Devil. And the Devil had the same ankle boots as Corporal Perlonghi, which is what Silvester saw in front of his nose when he, a recruit, was stretched out on the ground, completing field exercises. And that's why, given his face, feet, and hands, Uncle Silvester knew without a doubt that this devil was the real one. And if he refused to make a deal with him it was because he wanted to demonstrate to him that he neither believed in nor thought about his possible existence.

No, this isn't the way to begin. It doesn't make sense. If what you want to do is tell the story of the fiber glass business, then you need to begin another way. From a different angle.

But wasn't it like that? The story about the Devil?

Yes, it was. But it belongs to another part of the story.

Well, then, where do I begin?

Just where you should begin. From the beginning. Begin with the story about the *knutt*.

That story has nothing to do with it.

Then begin with the story about Pucho's first wife. That has something to do with it.

Aunt Judith says Pucho's first wife would always get her hair done in a perm. Even her pubic hair.

Aunt Clara says it isn't true because when Pucho's first wife married Pucho no one got permanents; instead, women wore shoulder-length hair with a forelock in the middle in the shape of a heart and two more, like little horns, on either side. Like baby horns or two peaks jutting out.

Aunt Judith says they used to do both: the erect forelock was in style then but there were others who got permanents.

Aunt Clara says maybe old women would get permanents, but Pucho's first wife was simply modern and up-to-date, and she became the very style she had chosen to use.

Aunt Judith says look who's calling the kettle black. If what Pucho's first wife used was the erect forelock and hair spray, Aunt Judith conceded, then she surely styled her pubic hairs into a forelock as well, and Clara must have used not only that forelock but even more to imitate her.

Everyone says Pucho's first wife was called Martita. Everyone says she was the twins' cousin from Down-the-Street, a solid fan of the

Rimetka Boys team, a great friend of Clara's when they were young girls, and Judith's best friend when they were older. And she was Silvester's confidant and friend and, at one time, his schoolmate at the university.

Everyone says Martita left Pucho and picked up with Sam Sim, a conductor of a tango orchestra that played at the Ferro Club. And ever since then, as far as the Rimetka family was concerned, Martita stopped being Martita and would always be known as Pucho's first wife.

What no one talks about is the fact that when Martita became a part of the Old House she brought happiness and after she was gone, she left only sadness.

What no one talks about but what everyone remembers is that Martita would help Aunt Judith meet with her secret boyfriend, who was later to become Uncle Ramón. And she would take Uncle Ramón's secret letters to Aunt Judith. And she would go window shopping with Clara and they had a barrel of fun during Carnaval spraying the street musicians with their perfume bottles. There was more than one night she stayed out studying with Silvester and his friends, which was before they threw him out of the university for political reasons, during the reign of the Long-tailed Devil. And even the Crazy-Lady-Around-the-Corner liked her because Martita wasn't afraid of her and, once in a while, when she was younger, she even played checkers with her.

Martita had green eyes and wasn't afraid of anybody or anything, and she wasn't afraid of Grandfather Gedalia either. Or even Judith. Martita studied law at a time when most woman didn't study at all. And when she came to live in the Old House as Pucho's wife, when he still wasn't able to buy or rent a house, she would listen to the news with Granny—whom she called Mom out of affection, yet spoke formally to her out of respect. And she spoke highly of her maté tea and Blanca Argentina's whipped mayonnaise.

And even Grandfather Gedalia didn't deign to look up from his pile of promissory notes and checks whenever Martita would enter his study in the Old House and say Dad to him and then invite him to go out to the movies in the evening and eat at the Roxy on Corrientes—which was the first self-service restaurant, located on Corrientes Street next to the Opera movie theater—and then have some ice cream at Tiky's, where you could get that soft, weird ice cream (with a topping) that would come out of a machine, and where you could even get an ice cream soda. Let's go to the movies and eat something afterward with Granny and Pucho, just the four of us, spend a little money, she would say to him, with a chuckle. As if it were possible, even believable, that Grandfather Gedalia would go out at night with Granny to blow money. And Grandfather Gedalia, who was then known as Dad, would laugh along with her, as if spending money was for him an appealing and a lighthearted joke. But he did it because it was for Martita.

Aunt Clara says it couldn't have been the Roxy because it opened long after Martita had left the country.

What no one understands is why Martita married Uncle Pucho.

Aunt Judith says when she thinks about Martita's harum-scarum ways—it's not often that Judith would use a softer word like *harum-scarum* instead of, for instance, "that horny bitch," which is more like her vocabulary, it's obvious that she, too, loved her a lot. She always remembers how amusingly she would dress, like wearing only one glove. She would wear a blue-and-white-striped sweater with one sleeve rolled down and the other rolled up (and it was on that arm that she would wear the glove that went past her elbow), pleats around the waist, buttons to one side, and a dark blue wool skirt. It wasn't a normal way of dressing, and it didn't suit everyone. It was one of those combinations that dressmakers call bold, the ones you see on mannequins or, at best, used by movie or radio actors for the purpose of making heads turn, that is, to create shock. One had to be courageous, like Martita was, to dress up like that on a typical Sunday and take a stroll down Florida Street.

What no one understands is why Martita didn't marry Silvester.

And whenever Judith thinks about her, she imagines her wearing that garb from back then, with that baby face, because when Martita took off with that orchestra director Sam Sim, she got a divorce and became legally married, after which they left for California and were never seen again. And the twins from Down-the-Block moved away and whenever someone would run into one of them on the street (but you could never be sure who was who) and even when they wouldn't ask, one of them would say something about Martita and her life in California, because it was only natural that the Rimetkas would want to know something about her but wouldn't dare ask.

What no one understands is how and why Martita married Uncle Pucho some six months after Silvester married The Dumb Turk. And there was that huge, spectacular reception which cost Grandfather Gedalia more than he had ever spent or ever would spend again because that era of putting on the dog was coming to an end and he was beginning to become, little by little, Mr. Tightwad.

Well, maybe so, but as far as I know Grandfather Gedalia only provided the house, and that famous reception was paid for by the father-in-law, The Dumb Turk's father.

Not so. Grandfather paid for it.

But hadn't you said the last big blowout in the Old House was Clara and Yaco's marriage reception?

That's all hearsay, stay out of it, let me tell it.

And The Book of Memories? What does it say?

I don't know. I can't find it. I don't know where I put it.

And Uncle Pucho still doesn't understand it, much less at the time. But then he began to realize that Martita was going to the Old House with the excuse to visit her friends more often than she normally would have and then he realized that suddenly Martita was smiling at him more than necessary, more than what she would normally do for others. Martita didn't smile much, not because she wasn't a friendly person, but because she had a gold cap on her upper left molar and she didn't like to expose it. Now she would brandish it at Pucho regularly, and when he saw what was going on, Pucho tried his best to rise to the occasion.

Because no one, absolutely no one, could understand why. What is not written in The Book of Memories, what no one talks about, but everyone wonders about, or, at least, they wondered at the time, is why, damn it (as Judith would say), didn't Silvester marry Martita.

But that's the way it went.

And Uncle Silvester, what does he say about Martita?

Uncle Silvester doesn't say a word. He says he doesn't remember and he always changes the subject.

Do you think I could stick in the part about the Devil here?

Be patient.

Uncle Silvester always acted upon his principles. Only when it was necessary did he adapt his principles to his actions.

But how could such a demanding and principled man also be a womanizer?

Because anything can happen in life.

Because it's not true.

Because one of his principles stated that he would not permit any woman to covet him in vain.

Not even his neighbor's wife?

Who knows?

Someone knows but no one is saying anything.

According to another one of his principles, he would not tell a lie. And he didn't. Many women who loved Silvester—his virility, his grey hats, his expert hands—could have complained about him. They may have felt sorrow and pain. But not one of them can say he deceived them.

We all boast about whatever we can.

And did he continue to chase women after he married The Turk?

The Dumb Turk? Aunt Judith says The Dumb Turk must have castrated him because after he married her, he turned into a monk.

Clara says Judith can't see beyond the nose on her face and, to top it off, she has that huge, crooked nose that prevents her from seeing anything. And after Silvester got married he never became a monk, he just became more discrete.

Uncle Pucho says The Turk is strong-willed, ignorant, but smart, and after getting married and with the passing of time and making more contacts, she became more refined, which was good for Uncle Silvester because she replaced certain notions about Trotsky floating around in his head and placed him squarely in the middle of the reality of life.

What is the reality of life like?

It's hard to explain, but it's something that has to do with making money.

And what does the matter of whether Uncle Silvester was a womanizer or not have to do with the story involving Uncle Pucho's first wife?

Nothing, it has nothing to do with it, don't you understand? Absolutely nothing. And don't even think about asking that stupid question again.

Now, then, let's talk about how each one of Grandfather Gedalia's children wanted independence. Because if we don't, we'll never get to the story about the fiber glass business.

Silvester and Pucho worked in their father's business. The cloth business. Because after being a peddler Grandfather Gedalia had a business in La Boca, the one with the Inundation Sales, and then he started a large cloth store on Alsina Street. He was the only Pole among all those Turks.

Grandfather Gedalia didn't like the idea of running a business on the street where there was so much thievery, especially involving the tax collectors, who are the biggest thieves of all. It was a business in which you had to pay employees and employee benefits (the ones that were imposed by the Long-tailed Devil) and an accountant who basically did nothing more than make annotations with an ink pen in a large accounting book when Gedalia could have done it himself with a pencil (a more practical method because you can erase the errors) in a simple oilcloth notebook.

Perhaps for that reason Grandfather never considered that business to be his primary one. Although he dealt in the cloth business, Grandfather Gedalia continued—like any artisan in love with his tools, his material, his work—with his old business. His business on Alsina Street was his last business and after Pucho ruined it, he dedicated himself to his other business.

But what was that?

It was loaning money, which seemed easy but it really wasn't; if it were, everyone who has money would be out loaning it.

Loaning money isn't hard, the hard part is getting people to pay it back with interest. That's why you have to know how to choose your clients well. That's why you have to know a lot of psychology, more than what Gastón knows, Aunt Clara's psychologist son.

The business on Alsina Street was really big.

Not that big.

It was so big it became a parking lot. They were importers: they brought silk and wool from England. High-quality stuff.

Grandfather Gedalia had a partner. Poor guy. When they went broke, his partner committed suicide which, in those times, is what you did. No one fought duels over their honor, but there were people who committed suicide over it.

It wasn't necessary for Grandfather Gedalia to commit suicide because by then he had nothing to do with the cloth store: after the problem with the postdated checks he saw it coming and so he sold his share when the other guy still had enough money to buy him out.

But if the business was going under, how was his partner able to buy him out?

No one knows how he did it, but everyone knows the poor guy would have sold his soul, wife, and three daughters in order to get out from under Grandfather Gedalia, who was driving him crazy.

And what did Grandfather Gedalia say when he found out he had committed suicide?

Grandfather Gedalia said you need to have faith, courage, and energy in life and if you don't have any of those qualities, you may as well not be living.

But that was much later on and we shouldn't mix things up or else nothing will make sense.

Where were we?

We were at the part where Pucho marries Martita, six months after Silvester marries The Dumb Turk.

And why did Silvester marry The Dumb Turk, may I ask?

Yes, you may ask. You may always ask.

And can you give me an answer?

It's not always possible to give an answer, but in this case, I can.

Aunt Judith says when you look at The Dumb Turk today you see a farting old lady with the look of a farting old lady, but when she married Silvester she was a beautiful lass, with piercing eyes and firm thighs, olive-colored skin with a honey-colored look, long hands and arched eyebrows, a raspy but sugary voice, three months pregnant, and well off financially.

Aunt Clara says Judith was always gossiping and believed that all women were like her and if The Turk had become pregnant three months before, why was it that six months later they still didn't have a child.

Aunt Judith says Aunt Clara is a good person, she's really good, so good that she's stupid, because if she doesn't remember the notorious hemorrhage that The Dumb Turk had during her honeymoon, then her head's full of camel shit. The Book of Memories states that Silvester and Fortunée went on their honeymoon to Bariloche, made a snowman, put a top hat on its head and a carrot for its nose. There's a photograph of it to prove it. You could look at it for hours without knowing whether the people in the picture were happy.

Grandfather Gedalia used to say parents shouldn't pay their children because they'll always owe their parents. Silvester and Pucho joined the business in order to learn about the realities of life and to pay for room and board in the Old House, plus their room and board ever since they were born. And if he gave them money, they weren't to consider it a salary: whatever the father has, so do the children; what's mine is yours and vice versa; to take care of the business is to take care of your inheritance, it's to your advantage, it's an indication of intelligence and an investment for the future.

So they wouldn't see it as a salary, Grandfather Gedalia gave them money like he would to a child. Whatever you need, Father Gedalia would say: whatever you need. Pucho and Silvester had to ask for money every time they needed it, explain what it was for, and then wait for their request to be granted. Money for the day: Grandfather Gedalia wouldn't advance them anything, not even for bus fare.

In order to fatten their wallets, they would resort to hitting up their mother, who didn't have much money either because Granny didn't get involved in money matters at all. Grandfather Gedalia personally took charge of buying most of the everyday things. For buying clothes and other stuff, there was always the *kuenteniks'* cooperative where they were still members and the wives could get merchandise they needed without having to pay money.

And that's the way Pucho and Silvester (and Clara and Judith as well) lived in the Old House, a place as big and beautiful as a castle, although a little run down, and there were times when they didn't have enough money even to buy candies.

If you want to study, then study, Grandfather Gedalia used to say, that doesn't do anybody any harm. But Pucho just didn't have a head for it and while Silvester did, he didn't use it right, and during the period of the Long-tailed Devil when he was an activist and participated in running the Student Center, they threw him out of the university, accusing him of being a Trotsky agitator (after learning from his dossier about the incident at the small socialist printing press).

And that's the reason, says Aunt Clara, why Silvester got married, that is, in order to become independent.

And that's the reason, says Aunt Judith, why Silvester went from a bad situation to a worse one, from the frying pan into the fire.

And that's the reason why poor Pucho had tried to get ahead with that secret which soon began to consume his energy, illusions, and desires, and then Martita's savings and the money he began to filch from the cloth store until the whole thing flew out the window, carried off in a wind storm on the wings of those infamous postdated checks.

The secret was neither some French hussy nor an obsession with gambling, as his brother and sisters originally thought; nope, it was the fiber glass business.

Because ever since Pucho got married, he would sleep in the Middle Room, with Martita in his arms, and he'd ask himself what he could do to make sure that dream would never end. Because it's no good to receive more than what one should receive and it's no good to have more than one needs, and Pucho loved Martita too much, more than a husband should love his wife. And Martita used to go to the university and she got along with everyone and she was good to Pucho, but being good to someone doesn't necessarily mean love and even Pucho realized the difference.

And now Pucho was getting a salary in the cloth store, but it wasn't enough to rent a house for his wife, not even a run-down apartment.

And Silvester had stopped working in the cloth store because he started working for his father-in-law in a small shop making copper wire and metal edging for decorated plates and later on, metal lining for the first transformers that were ever produced in the country. It slowly went from a small shop to a factory and, in time, his children began calling it the Metal Box Factory.

And some say Silvester slept with the female workers and the office staff and drove everyone hard, and others say only men worked in the factory and everyone says Silvester had a good mind for industry and his father-in-law didn't.

But Pucho continued working in the cloth store and he kept the fiber glass factory a secret until the very end (or that's what he believed anyway). And that's why anyone could have confused the business with his interest in some woman or gambling, even though it was something totally different.

Pucho called it the Acoustic Coating Company (and that was the correct name for it, even though he himself thought it sounded high-falutin in relation to the modesty of the operation itself). Specifically, it consisted of an old, rented house which was used in part for storage, with massive sheets of fiber glass stacked against the walls, so near-looking to cotton and snow that you always wanted to touch it, but you weren't supposed to because everyone knew that it hurt your hands: the little slivers would get stuck in your skin and if they get into a vein they could travel to your heart and you'd die.

Fiber glass was used as insulation for walls and ceilings. In the storage area, where there were some large tables, two or three workers who used protective gloves would stick the fiber glass into long bags and sew them up. They looked like mattresses. Then they would put the mattresses in some wooden frames that, in turn, became the ceilings for houses or buildings. In order to block the glitter of the fiber glass, they covered it with that old Kraft paper which had been blackened with tar, or what they originally called rubber oil.

Potential customers would look at the fiber glass brand with the long fibers, which was the best, and they would say: "But this material is noxious."

"Not in the least," Pucho would tell them. "It has nothing noxious about it. You can handle it with no problem. Watch."

And in order to prove what he was saying, he would grab a big handful of fiber glass, squeeze it, and juggle it back and forth from hand to hand.

Fiber glass is made like cotton candy: they spin silica powder under heat in a metal dish and the centrifugal force produces the fiber glass material. Sometimes, though, the speed of the spinning slows down, or for some reason or other they have to turn off the machine and then turn it back on again, or sometimes the temperature goes down and, instead of forming that cotton candy texture, sharp pieces of glass are created. When Pucho would energetically juggle the fiber glass from hand to hand, trying to demonstrate that the material was totally inoffensive, he always got slivers in his hands and oftentimes he would end up cutting himself.

"Completely safe, you see," Pucho would tell them, and then he'd continue talking to them with a bloody hand stuck inside his pocket. "In fact, it's better than the fiber made from basalt."

And like so many companies and small-time operations that got started in the country, the fiber glass business was a very profitable one, but not everyone who got into it was successful. Pucho got into the business too late in the game, when some larger companies had already established a foothold and had become major suppliers.

And, in addition, in order to be successful in a business venture, you've got to be strong and know when to say no.

And Aunt Judith says Pucho was never very strong and, on top of it all, he got involved with that piece of shit for a business partner, who stunk worse than a drunk's vomit, and using the excuse that Pucho shouldn't be involved in the business that much because he had to work in the cloth store, all the while, he was screwing him over royally.

And when the business started to go under, Pucho got involved with moneylenders which is the worst thing you could do.

Moneylenders are the worst thing?

No, moneylenders are just fine. They do their job. To get involved with moneylenders is the worst thing you can do.

And then, at the lowest point of his life (and that's saying a lot, considering that there were many, many low points in his life), when the fiber glass business was going to hell and Silvester was forced to go to the police because of the bad checks and, as much as he tried to hide it, Grandfather Gedalia had begun to realize something strange was going on as well (and if it hadn't caused a ruckus it was because he had already planned his exit from the cloth store and he didn't want to reveal his secret to his partner), and when Pucho felt life was playing against him, scoring a terrible goal, and when he was beginning to go bald, despite being a young man, Pucho was walking down Rivadavia Street one afternoon and had the unfortunate idea to look in the window of a pastry shop at the area reserved for families. . . .

I can't continue, a page is missing.

It's missing or was it torn out?

Six of one, half dozen of another.

So, may I tell the part about Uncle Silvester and the Devil here?

Nope. It doesn't go here. That had already occurred long before. More or less a month after Martita and Pucho got married.

And you didn't let me know so I could tell it?

I didn't because there are things that shouldn't be told or imagined. If it's not in The Book of Memories, there must be a reason for it. It must be something that's not worth remembering.

But can't you ask about it?

You can ask anything you want. But you won't always get an answer.

I want to know if Pucho signed a pact with the Devil.

He didn't sign anything. In order to get whatever he wanted, Pucho never needed any Devil. Back then, thank God, he wasn't any dirty old man like Dr. Faust, no, he was a handsome young man who used that Brill Cream you don't find anymore.

So, what happened?

Well, it so happened that Pucho, after seeing what was up, decided to go all the way, which was to set fire to the fiber glass business, collect the insurance money, and move to another country.

Where?

It could have been Rio de Janeiro or it could have been New York or it could have been Córdoba.

With or without Martita?

With or without Martita.

And then what happened?

Well, one Saturday morning Pucho bought two containers of kerosene and that same afternoon he took them to the fiber glass shop.

Fiber glass used for acoustic insulation had a big advantage. It wouldn't burn.

Of course, Pucho was well aware of it. But the Kraft paper slopped in tar was like an explosive. And there were the wooden frames as well. And the mattress cloth. Even though it wouldn't burn, the fiber glass would be destroyed when it melted with the heat.

It happened on a winter afternoon when it was cold and sunny. Pucho went to the patio at the back of the rented house carrying a kerosene can in each hand. They were heavy and the metal handles left marks in his hands. And he had to struggle to get the lids off. That's the way it was and will always be. Nothing was ever easy for Pucho.

He stood there for a while, not knowing where to begin, then he splashed kerosene all over the wood frames, the wrapping, the rubber oil and, finally, the floor and walls. Then he took a box of matches out of his pocket and lit one.

Then he blew it out. Then he lit another one, then he blew it out. And then he realized that to set fire to the business was going to be a big fucking mistake. A huge fucking mistake. And he was just some poor jerk who was unable to do anything right and, above all, anything big. He couldn't even make a big fucking mistake right.

He had left the front door open and all of a sudden he heard Silvester's voice. He had come in quietly and was standing directly behind Pucho.

"What cha doin, dimwit," Silvester said, calmly, blowing smoke from one of his cigarettes.

"You're the dimwit," Pucho said. "Put out that cigarette or else we're all going up in flames."

"If you had taken high school chemistry, you'd know that you're wasting kerosene by throwing it on top of tar.

Nevertheless, Pucho really loved his brother Silvester. But chemistry was the very course that had stopped him in his tracks from graduating from high school.

What do you mean by "nevertheless"?

Everyone's susceptible to something and has his own Achilles' heel, like Granny used to say, and Pucho could suffer any kind of humiliation, but not this: the memory of high school chemistry, especially at that moment when he was so nervous.

Nevertheless, what?

Shut up, OK? Shut up and listen. What I'm telling you is that when Pucho heard "chemistry class," he just blew up and jumped all over Silvester and they went at it like never before, even though they weren't used to fighting like that. They laid into each other, but not really, there were those muffled blows until Silvester fell down, pulling Pucho with him, and they rolled on the floor and Pucho's face rubbed up against a pile of fiber glass. And nothing happened, except that the two of them got scared enough to stop the fight.

"How did you know I was here?" Pucho asked.

"I followed you. Not today. The other day. I wanted to know who your sex-crazed French lady was."

"There she is. Like her?"

"Hey, brother, it's not worth it."

Then Pucho hugged Silvester with all his heart and started crying. And Silvester, who was uneasy, patted him on the back of his thick sport coat made of white and black herringbone tweed. He patted Pucho on the back and held his arms and didn't know how to get loose from him.

Then Pucho let go of his brother and sat down on a stool.

And Silvester was just about to stretch out on a pile of fiber glass that seemed so soft and fluffy, but Pucho stopped him just in time.

And Pucho, who was a lot younger, remembered something that had happened many years ago. He remembered when Silvester first began going out at night, and he didn't want him to go out alone, so he wanted to go with his big brother no matter what, or make him stay at home. And he would begin to cry. Then Silvester would pat him on the head and promise he'd be back, and he'd give him his ID. And Pucho would fiercely clutch that ID with Silvester's picture on it and Mommy (Granny) would take him to her big bed because she was always afraid he'd have an asthma attack. And he'd go to sleep squeezing that ID in his hand.

And Pucho, flooded with memories, wave after wave of warm memories that erased his fury and his embarrassment and the tension, leaving his knees weak and making him want to urinate badly, watching his brother Silvester who was just standing there not knowing what to say or do, feeling deeply stupid, remembered the picture on the ID that would allow him to go to sleep, a picture of that other Silvester, the young guy whose beard hadn't started to grow. Then he said:

"Why don't you go straight to fucking hell. You were always shitting on me. You made me eat soap when I didn't want to play soccer."

"That's a lie. When did I ever . . .," Silvester said. "When did I ever make you eat soap?"

"You threatened to."

"But it never occurred to me to do it."

"And how was I to know?" said Pucho. "To me it was the same as making me really eat it. I'm going to tell my children that my brother made me eat soap."

And afterward they went to the corner bar to have a drink, which is what they liked to do, both of them being the Rimetkas who liked to eat and drink. However, they were unaware that during the fight Silvester's cigarette had popped out of his mouth and fallen into a corner of the patio. It would have gone out by itself if it had not been for the fact that it fell on a piece of newspaper which caught on fire.

The flaming piece of newspaper lifted into the air ever so gently and fell into an area awash with kerosene and tar. The fire department came and kept the blaze under control and evacuated the neighbors, but the fiber glass business went up in smoke.

And the insurance company did an investigation and found the cans of kerosene—or the remains of them—and declared that the fire was set intentionally and, fortunately, they didn't put Pucho in jail, but they didn't pay one red cent of insurance money either.

And it wasn't long after the fiber glass business that Grandfather Gedalia got out of the cloth business and Martita left the Rimetka family for that Sam Sim, or Samuel Siminovich, the director of the band that played at Ferro's dance hall.

Clara and Her First Baby

Clara, sitting in her new, pretty but rented apartment, looks out the window and takes in the sounds coming in from the outside. They're not facing the street. The street is a ways away because the building is located on a narrow but deep piece of land. Clara's apartment is on the second floor (this is the Period of Condominiums and, just about everyone who can afford to buy housing purchases apartments in buildings that are under construction or, in fact, still only a project). Off in the distance, she can make out a part of Rivadavia Park—the swings and the big eucalyptus tree—from the only window of the apartment that looks out onto the street.

What do you mean Clara was living in a rented apartment? But didn't Uncle Yaco always have a lot of money?

Uncle Yaco had a lot of money when he married Clara, but he lost it and then he turned around and got it back.

The part outside the apartment that interests Clara (who is young but not particularly pretty) is the hallway and the elevator. She wants to get to the door before her guests arrive so the doorbell won't wake up the baby. It took a lot to get him to sleep, and she likes him more when he's asleep than awake.

Clara is getting terribly fat, but she doesn't care because she believes that as soon as she stops breast-feeding she will begin a rigorous diet that will make her lose weight quickly. Her friends have recommended a dietary specialist, Dr. Gdansk, who prescribes a concoction in capsules that never fails.

But what's going to happen is just the opposite: Clara is going to get fatter and fatter, until finally she has those wrists with rolls of fat in between which her bracelets are hidden, the same wrists that her baby has today. It's better not to know. Why learn about one's fate when it's impossible to change?

That's the problem of viewing the facts from afar, looking backwards, trying to face our memories. Every decision that at one point seemed to be driven by one's free will have become fused, now stuck together with the glue of time, to make up an irreversible destiny that seems to have been set in cement since the beginning of time. You have to make an effort to remember that each instant of those lives could have been different. The choices were for real and there was more than one predetermined road ahead.

Even though Clara waits nervously, the visitors arrive, of course, while she's in the bathroom and the doorbell rings long and loudly, waking up the baby. Only Clara's father is capable of ringing the bell like that, as if he were trying to knock down the door with just the force of the ringing.

"And did he go poopoo today," asks the one who has finally become, for the first time, Grandfather Gedalia.

Granny follows him in but doesn't say a word. She gives Clara a

kiss and takes some warm cookies wrapped in paper and a jar of home-
made marmalade out of her purse. The cookies smell wonderful, because they're fresh, but you could tell they were made with vegetable
oil. After arriving to the promised land so many years ago, Granny
still considers butter an unnecessary luxury. Looking ahead, the future seems open-ended; looking backwards, through memory, everything happened so fast.

"He's already gone poopoo, Daddy," Clara says. There's a note of
weariness in her voice. The baby was born less than a month ago, a
Caesarean birth, one of the first of its type in all of Argentina. Sometimes Clara looks at herself in the mirror and sees that large, red scar
that travels downward from her navel, bisecting her abdomen into
two flaccid parts.

"What color was it?"

"Yellow, Daddy."

While she talks, Clara rocks the little crib by pushing it back and
forth on its wheels. The baby continues to cry. Clara vaguely remembers the old-fashioned cribs that mothers could rock with their foot
while they sewed or cooked or embroidered. Grandfather Gedalia talks
about the importance of the diverse colors that a baby's stool can
have according to the baby's health. It's obvious that he is talking
about theories that haven't been proven. Furtively, Clara and Granny
look at each other with skepticism.

"You shouldn't rock him because it will spoil him," Granny says.

"I'd like to have a shot of whiskey," says Grandfather Gedalia, "but
not that kind. The imported stuff. I want some from the bottle your
husband has hidden so you won't have to offer me any."

Clara wants to do everything right. She wants to be a good daughter and a good wife and a good mother. Until now, Clara has always
done things right. That's why it's not fair she isn't happy. Now she
wants to serve her father that glass of whiskey and then set the table

nicely for tea. When Clara was engaged, her father called her husband by his name instead of what he says now, "your husband." The baby starts to scream.

Was Clara so poor she couldn't afford a maid?

She wasn't that poor. Maids were given Thursday afternoons and Sundays off. That day was a Thursday afternoon and the maid was at a nearby park with her boyfriend.

Did Aunt Clara get married because she was in love or was it for convenience?

Aunt Clara got married because she was in love, but not with her husband, rather with her father, and the one who wanted to see her married was Grandfather Gedalia.

"That baby's hungry," Granny says.

"And two cubes of ice," Grandfather Gedalia says.

As he cries, the baby's face becomes constricted and turns red. In a way it's better to see him like that instead of when he's serene and relaxed. His cheeks are always too red, as if he were exploding with anger, and his eyes seem strange, too. Be it fortune or misfortune, as a part of his Down's syndrome, he has a genetic heart disease that would soon end his life. In less than a year he'd be dead. Death will have overtaken him painlessly, in his sleep. There was not only no picture of him, but also no mention of his name in The Book of Memories. As if he was always known as the baby, that baby.

But didn't Clara have another baby?

Then she had her psychologist baby, a real psychologist, one of the first psychologists around, not like nowadays where there are more psychologists than everyone put together. And who knows how professional they are, but that's why the profession is the way it is, it's losing ground, and intelligent people don't go to psychologists like they used to. When Aunt Clara's son graduated from the university in Rosario, psychology had just been invented, and at the time no one even knew if it was a profession. Engineering is a profession, Granny used to say, but she wasn't sure about architecture; medicine is a profession, but she wasn't sure about psychology. A dentist was a professional, but not as much as a doctor.

Granny lifts the baby into her arms and puts him face down across her knees, rocking him. The baby stops crying.

"This is the way you do it," she tells Clara. "The problem is you're too sensitive. See, he calmed down immediately with me. I have experience."

Clara, who is in the kitchen, has problems with the metal ice tray. The water isn't hot enough to get the cubes out. Clara bangs the tray against the counter top.

"That girl is really nervous," Grandfather Gedalia says.

"Young people have no patience," says Granny, who feels too young to be a grandmother although she won't admit it. "Why isn't the servant here, Clara?"

"We don't say servant anymore, we say maid. Today is Thursday."

"Thursday. Bah. You don't know how to treat her, you know. That girl is going to take advantage of you. She already has."

The baby doesn't have much hair but it's combed so that a ringlet like a wave stands up on the top of his head. As a demonstration of being modern, she let him be shaved when he was born. However, now she combs his hair the normal way.

Everybody treats him as if he were a normal baby. What else could they do? Grandfather Gedalia, nevertheless, doesn't touch him.

And where's Uncle Yaco?

Today's a work day. Uncle Yaco is at the store, working.

Why did Aunt Clara marry Uncle Yaco?

It was a real blowout, a party to end all parties. At the Old House. It was just before the Crash and it was the last time Grandfather Gedalia wanted to splurge.

I'm not asking about that. I'm asking why did Aunt Clara marry Uncle Yaco. Why?

Why? No one knows. What is known is that Uncle Yaco was one of the last men in the city to stop wearing a hat. What is also known is that he used to come to the Old House to visit Clara and upon leaving there would always be a folded piece of paper in his hat band. Once out on the street Yaco would unfold the piece of paper which always said the same thing: "Don't come back."

And who would put the piece of paper in his hat band?

No one knows that either.

And he just kept coming back?

He kept coming because he was a friend of Grandfather Gedalia's. He would visit Clara and play dominoes with Grandfather Gedalia. Clara also played dominoes. But no one could beat Grandfather Gedalia.

Clara has managed to get the ice out of the tray. She pours the whiskey and takes it to her father. The baby is crying again.

"This baby's hungry," Granny says.

"But he just ate, Mom, he ate and went to sleep just before you came."

"And he wants to eat again!"

"Do you have any olives? Some cheese?" Grandfather Gedalia asks.

"But Daddy, I was going to serve tea."

"I'm drinking whiskey. Whiskey doesn't go with tea."

Grandfather Gedalia says, "That baby's stomach is hurting. It's a shame there's not a comfortable armchair in this house."

"There's not even a comfortable chair," Granny says.

The baby cries.

Clara got married the old way, she married a rich, older man. Her marriage was one of Grandfather Gedalia's business ventures that had turned out just fine. Since then, Clara's purpose in life is to show the world she is a modern, up-to-date, open-minded woman, ready to accept innovation and change. Consequently, she was the first of the Rimetka family to reject the false French style and to decorate her apartment (that enormous apartment on Libertador that they had to sell later) in false Scandinavian that seems terribly uncomfortable.

Clara and Yaco didn't have a television set in their big apartment on Libertador because television didn't exist then.

They don't have one in the apartment on Caballito because it's an expensive novelty. In their next apartment, on Alvear Avenue, they will have a television set, built into a Scandinavian-designed entertainment center, a special piece of furniture (always Scandinavian) that also has a place for the radio and record player and several very practical drawers that are never neat and orderly.

"That baby's hungry," Granny says.

Clara doesn't have the strength to continue resisting. She goes to the bedroom. She opens the front part of her dress, undoes her brassiere, and lets the baby latch onto her nipple. The baby stops crying and sucks enthusiastically.

Clara feels like her baby has let her down, acting contrary to the best expected of him in front of her parents, and she doesn't know whether to love him in desperation or hope that he dies. The baby sucks and she feels something, something vital, flowing from her nipples into that little body that's growing at her expense. Every time the baby sucks, Clara feels like crying.

"I told you so," Granny says. "That baby was hungry. I have experience. But don't bend over too much while he sucks or else your back is going to hurt. It's better to sit on a little stool."

"An old man has the right to ask for some olives," Grandfather Gedalia says loudly from the living room. "He's got a right to have a little cheese, too." He's only joking, of course, but only half joking and the two women know it very well.

Aunt Judith says Clara's famous stuffed armchairs were nothing more than traps, ass-trappers: once you sit down in one of those things, it's like being stuck there and then you have to ask someone to pull you out.

Uncle Pucho says Aunt Judith was always a vulgar person and Aunt Clara, on the other hand, was always a refined person. She had good taste, she knew how to dress as well as to decorate her house.

Uncle Silvester says Aunt Clara's Scandinavian furniture was a little strange but very modern and, in fact, after many years it still continued to be modern. It's just that he prefers the French style because it's more prestigious looking.

The Book of Memories says Aunt Clara's husband had a comfortable armchair that was neither modern nor matched the rest of the furniture. It was his armchair, one that he had brought from his parent's house and put in the bedroom. Then he let his wife choose whatever she wanted for the rest of the house, just so long as she would let him sit down and calmly read the newspaper in his armchair.

Several (but no one knows who) say that in addition to an armchair he also had a lover, a married woman who was even at Clara's wedding with her husband, and that Uncle Yaco had taken them with him to the wedding and almost—but not quite—put her in his bedroom along with the armchair.

The baby goes to sleep while he sucks. Clara realizes she should change him, but she doesn't want to wake him up again. She carefully puts him on his side in the rocker. When her psychologist son has children he's going to put them to sleep face down because that's what the pediatrician recommends. It will be difficult for Clara to accept the idea that babies won't suffocate that way. Just as it's hard for Granny to accept the idea that they don't need to be tightly wrapped anymore, just diapers and the navel bandage—that long piece of gauze that goes around their waists—are enough.

"Have you seen Judith lately?" Granny asks her in a hushed voice.

"She came by yesterday. She's doing fine," Clara says. "She sends you a big kiss."

And Clara asks herself again where she went wrong. Why this, if she had done everything they wanted her to? Why this, if she had always been a good daughter, the one for whom her mother and father always had a soft spot, she never swore and didn't even get married for love? Why hasn't she received just compensation in life, the reward she deserves, a little bit of happiness, or something vaguely related to being happy?

"How much do you think your husband has lost this past month?" Grandfather Gedalia asks, eating some olives. "These are pure seeds. Too small. You don't know how to shop. It's easy to cheat you. You've got to buy larger, juicier olives. How much did you pay for this crap?"

"I think things went better this month," Clara says.

"The cheese is too warm. He came out ahead? Even taking out the rent for the store?"

"Well, the store is ours, we don't pay rent. You're supposed to eat the cheese at room temperature, you don't have to put it in the refrigerator."

"You don't eat warm cheese. Not exactly. You've got to calculate the rent."

And Aunt Clara, did she love her husband?

She did when she married him, more or less. But afterward, when his business started to go downhill, she loved him a lot more. Because then she had a better opportunity to demonstrate that she hadn't married out of convenience.

When Uncle Yaco's business was about to go under, Aunt Clara loved him even more, from morning until night. And when Uncle Yaco's business started to flourish again, Aunt Clara had already demonstrated how much she loved him, so she didn't have to continue whipping mayonnaise. Aunt Clara thought whipping mayonnaise was an act of love.

When Uncle Yaco got rich again and they abandoned the rented apartment on Caballito and bought the big apartment on Alvear

Avenue, Aunt Clara was devoting one hundred percent of her time to their second child, Gastón, her psychologist child.

Clara didn't set out a nice table for tea. She made maté tea and shared it with Granny. Drinking out of the old gourd gave her a feeling of solace, as if she herself were—for a few moments—a baby. She didn't even put the cookies on a plate: she was devouring them straight from the grease-stained brown paper bag. Given the way Clara is, her actions were surprising and indicated a serious change in her spirits. Granny recognized it and gently patted her hand.

When Clara got married, her husband was twenty years older than she was.

And now?

Now it's much less. In time, the differences become less, everything changes. Since he was so much older than she, when she was younger, Uncle Yaco treated her like a little girl. On the one hand, he gave her everything she wanted but, on the other, he didn't respect her much.

When Clara got big and fat, he still treated her like a little girl.

"What's wrong?" Granny asks her finally, not because she really wants to know, but because of the overly abundant way in which Clara is devouring the cookies. Grandfather Gedalia reads the newspaper with ferocious enthusiasm.

"Nothing. There's nothing wrong with me. I thought you were going to bring me something."

"Bring you something? We did," Granny says, pointing to the cookies and the marmalade.

"Something for the baby. For your grandson! Your first grandson!" Clara says, raising her voice. Even though she might yell at her mother, her fury is directed at her father, but she knows she can't yell at him directly.

"Something? Like what?"

"Anything. Whatever. Pajamas. A rattle. But you won't spend money on anything. Aren't you rich enough to buy a rattle?"

"My dear child," Grandfather Gedalia pronounces with much patience (and Clara remembers it's the same tone her husband uses with her), "my child, why do you want a rattle? It's not worth it: a rattle gets broken, you throw it away. It's not much money, but it's money wasted. You shouldn't throw money away, even if it's a little bit. You want some noise for your baby? Listen."

Grandfather Gedalia takes out his key chain and gently shakes it, making the keys jingle. Frankly, they sound pretty good, and if the baby had been awake he probably would have been listening attentively and soon he would be reaching out to grab the keys. In order to demonstrate all of the possibilities of the improvised toy, Grandfather Gedalia holds the key chain in such a way that a ray of sunlight is reflected off a key and projected onto the wall. Clara is trembling and her voice is drowned in anguish and rage. There's no direct relationship between the intensity of her feelings and the motives that provoked them.

"They're dirty," she says, "don't you realize that those stupid keys are dirty. How could you give them to a baby?"

"A rattle also gets dirty," says Grandfather Gedalia. "It falls to the floor, it gets thrown around, everyone touches it, no one ever washes it. A rattle gets dirty and so does a baby."

"A rattle can be washed!"

"You can also wash a key chain. Do want me to show you how?" As Grandfather Gedalia begins to get up, Clara knows full well she won't be able to take watching him wash the key chain in the bathroom sink, so she doesn't let him get up. Her father's logic is impeccable and it takes her away from the source of her anguish.

"You're not capable of giving anything to your grandson. Absolutely nothing!"

"That's where you're quite wrong," Granny says, "that's why you'll have to learn to understand your father better: he doesn't like to give useless gifts. And of course we brought something for our grandchild! Something worthwhile! Something valuable!"

Then Grandfather Gedalia mumbles some numbers and takes a big envelope from inside his jacket pocket and gives it to Clara, who then takes a deep breath trying to control herself. Now she's even more upset and embarrassed about having so little faith; nevertheless, and without being able to think about it, she notices the bulge in the envelope. All small bills?

"Open it," Grandfather Gedalia says, "open it and see for yourself."

Clara opens the envelope and discovers the amount he muttered was distributed in the following way: ten percent local currency, ten percent in dollars, and eighty percent in different kinds of checks from different parts of the country, postdated for cashing from 60 to 180 days from then. Clara begins to laugh with an ugly, nervous smile that she's unable to control.

"I told you this girl is a little nervous today," Grandfather Gedalia says.

"This isn't what you call nervousness, it's what you call mental exhaustion. My dear little Clara, light of my life, have you seen a doctor?"

Clara nods affirmatively with her head because she's unable to talk. She goes to the bathroom and looks for some pills in the medicine cabinet. She swallows one with some sparkling water. The pill dissolves on her tongue, leaving a bitter taste. It's hard for her to swallow it. Then she takes a spoonful of her mother's strawberry jam that tastes like it's been burned.

When she returns from the kitchen, her parents are getting ready to leave. She thanks them for the gift and says goodbye.

That night Clara and Yaco dump the contents of the envelope onto the dining room table and classify the checks according to the date and where they're from. They try to calculate the approximate amount of money they'll get after paying commissions and, above all, a percentage for cashing them. Nevertheless, it's a good amount of money and they can use it.

At 11:15 Pucho's second wife calls on the phone asking for help because her husband hasn't returned home during the whole day and she doesn't know where he is.

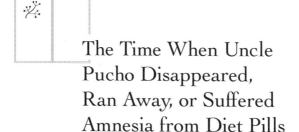

The Time When Uncle Pucho Disappeared, Ran Away, or Suffered Amnesia from Diet Pills

While Pucho's second wife (the one who was cut up into pieces) would speak, her mouth always became a little twisted to the left side. As a result, whatever she said seemed to be tinged with irony, as if everything had a double meaning that the person listening to her had to decipher.

Partially smiling with that look of needing an accomplice, Pucho's second wife complained so much and so often that you wished finally she had a reason like other people to complain. On the one hand, many who had wished it ended up regretting it later, after they had begun to cut her up into pieces; on the other hand, they didn't regret it at all that first night when Pucho was nowhere to be found.

In her long war with Granny, Pucho's second wife was gaining ground, conquering more and more territory from her headquarters in the Room-Halfway-Down-the-Hall. She had been so successful that Aunt Clara could finally say she didn't know who was living in whose house, and all she wanted to do was visit her mother's house (which had been her house and still continued to be her house) but, in reality, she was in her sister-in-law's house (which wasn't her house or anything).

Nonchalantly, as if she were talking about something else, or another person, or some other situation that wasn't necessarily her own, she, Pucho's second wife, would comment that heaven help the woman who would be so unfortunate as to have to live in someone else's house and have to put up with the in-laws and their meddling with raising her children; or if a woman were to be so unfortunate not to have married a man who is in a position to take her away from that crappy house with the damp walls and ceilings so high you had to tie three long feather dusters together in order to reach the cobwebs, and who— that same man—wouldn't take you to live in a place where you could enjoy your own privacy and whip mayonnaise in peace without anyone standing over you and trying to vex you.

And, no doubt, there was the delicate matter of Pucho's sexual prowess: not only could he not have children (The Indian Girl had been adopted) and no one knew who was at fault, but also he had been suspiciously abandoned by that crazy woman (the loved one, The-One-Who-Isn't-Mentioned), the one who fell in love with the orchestra director who usually played at the Ferro Club, where Uncle Pucho used to take her during Carnaval.

The Book of Memories doesn't usually contain the thoughts or feelings of anyone, or much information about their "true character," but there are exceptions. It states clearly there that Uncle Pucho's three siblings, plus his mother, Elvira, and Blanca Argentina (the two maids who worked and fought with each other in the Old House after the Crash, one of whom sided with Pucho's wife and the other with Granny), hoped Uncle Pucho had escaped.

The day Pucho didn't return home, his second wife got worried by lunchtime when her husband, knowing she was going to fix a Russian salad, didn't show up as he always did and take a big spoonful directly from the bowl instead of serving it on a plate. Nevertheless (that's what she told Clara anyway), she tried to remain calm, thinking that Pucho had finally decided to take his dieting seriously.

Uncle Pucho, who was very fat, had gone to see a dietitian recommended by his sister Clara. This doctor required a large battery of tests—an analysis of glucose levels, a gastrointestinal series, and a basic metabolism exam. But he always ended up prescribing some diet pills (in reality they weren't pills but capsules containing a powder mixture) that he gave in exactly the same proportions to all of his patients. They made Uncle Pucho feel rotten. Uncle Pucho called the diet pills torpedoes: Dr. Gdansk's famous torpedoes.

If Granny wasn't worried at lunchtime it's because she was always worried. Something horrible could occur at any moment. In fact, something horrible was occurring in some part of the world at that very moment; in fact, something horrible would always happen to the people she loved (like getting married, for instance). Granny used to say that some people are born with pot bellies and others just have bad luck and what all that means is that we can't predict our future because it's already preordained. And she wanted to express it with a proverb but she always got it backwards in Spanish. And she had not only Aunt Judith in mind when she talked about bad luck, since things had not gone right for her in life, but also the entire family, because it had been an unlucky family, except when Grandfather Gedalia won the lottery with the same number that he had chosen all his life, five years after his death.

And Granny was right, for you didn't even have to look beyond poor Pucho, one of whose two wives left him for that Sam Sim and the second one, over time, ended up being cut up into tiny pieces by the doctors: first one of her breasts, then a piece of her lung, and so on, one operation after another.

And due to that bad luck, it seems like Uncle Pucho, or perhaps it was his second wife, was unable to have children. And that's why they adopted The Indian Girl when she was just a baby. And they never once mentioned that she had been adopted until it was discovered after she was older, which is when all hell broke loose. That was when Aunt Clara stated that they should have told her when she was small, because to hide something is always bad and everything should always be brought out into the open. But when the child was small, and so beautiful and swarthy looking, she began to stand out in that Polish family (it was Aunt Judith who coined her nickname). It would have never occurred to Aunt Clara to say something about it and if it occurred to her now it's because she spoke through the eyes of her psychologist son and because she wanted to show everyone she didn't have a caveman mentality.

Without pointing a finger, Aunt Judith used to say there were not only intelligent cavemen but also, in this supersonic age today, people with their heads up their asses.

One thing for certain is that when Uncle Pucho escaped, got lost, or suffered amnesia from Gdansk's torpedoes, it wasn't necessary to say anything to Granny about it because she was always the first one to say something. And it wasn't necessary to hide anything from Grandfather Gedalia because he never found out about things he didn't like to know about.

Grandfather had an almost elegant way of playing stupid that made it hard to believe he was born in that small village in Poland where in the spring the snow would melt and turn the streets into mudholes. When Uncle Pucho didn't return to the Old House that night and no one knew where he was, not even his wife (or, better yet, especially his wife), everyone thought it wasn't necessary for Grandfather to find out about it. Everyone collaborated together in order to keep it a secret. It was similar to when he woke up after his Collapse and said, "Hi, how are you?" to Aunt Judith who was sitting next to his bed, some seventeen years after he had literally thrown her out of the Old House. Similarly, with that same skill, he actively went out of his way not to find out what was going on with poor Pucho.

On the other hand, some years before when Uncle Pucho hadn't shown up one night because he was in jail for those postdated checks, Grandfather Gedalia found out immediately and thought that was the end for him. Grandfather Gedalia was always ready to face the worst and that time it was difficult for Clara and Silvester to convince him that if he continued burying his children alive he was going to end up old and solitary.

And it was so good, Clara used to say, Grandfather Gedalia loosened up (concerning the postdated checks and the fiber glass disaster) and forgave Uncle Pucho, because many years later he and his daughter came to be the light of his life after both Granny and Pucho's second wife had died and Grandfather Gedalia was too old to walk with a cane and had to hold on to the back of a chair to get around.

(That bastard, Aunt Judith would say, didn't deserve getting any attention, especially the way those idiots Pucho and his daughter even made sure his balls got sprinkled with talcum powder. That's the way she put it, as if she weren't at all a little bit jealous of The Indian Girl who was in charge of powdering Grandfather Gedalia's crusty skin on his ass.)

Pucho's daughter was still really young the night he didn't return home to sleep next to her mother in the Room-Halfway-Down-the-Hall in the Old House. And that's what they called her: The Indian Girl, except for her mother who called her Alice. They gave her the same excuse that they gave Grandfather Gedalia: just as they couldn't deceive him, they couldn't really pull the wool over her eyes either.

And so when Uncle Pucho got lost, escaped, or suffered from amnesia due to Gdansk's torpedoes, Granny was the first one to realize what had happened, his wife was second, the third was his daughter, and then they told his brother and sister, Silvester and Clara, both of whom were married by then and didn't live in the Old House anymore. That first night they didn't call Aunt Judith because her relationship with the family was still pretty unstable and no one had the gumption to ask her to help them find Uncle Pucho; anyway, he wasn't, precisely, her favorite brother either.

The first day they spent looking for him they made telephone calls and personal visits; the second day they used Silvester's method; the third day they informed Judith, and then they went to see Clara's palm reader.

Aunt Clara said her medium was the best there ever was and she had known a bunch of them over the years, most of whom were cheating liars because they only told you what you wanted to hear, but with Miss Blackie she'd give you the bad news straight to your face.

Aunt Judith said they didn't tell her about it right away because ever since she had married Uncle Ramón her own brothers and sister treated her as if she had leprosy, and as fortunetellers go, they could have sought out her medium since she was so good at discovering lost things. For instance, she was the one who knew where the pearl was after that necklace broke, and, similarly, she would be able to find her brother Pucho—no matter how much he differed from a pearl.

Aunt Clara said the person Aunt Judith had recommended so highly was just a good business person and when she went to see her once because she had personal problems that she hadn't planned on revealing, that medium ended up giving her a recipe for tomato marmalade for her circulation problems. Well, she never even had circulation problems and, to top it off, the marmalade was horrible.

But by that terrible third day, the same day the Rimetka siblings went to visit the medium, the strangest part of all that made them look at each other with astonishment and desperation was to realize Silvester was inside a fortune-teller's house. It could've been anyone else but not Silvester; he didn't believe in God or the Devil, or religion or anything, he even disliked the Hebrew Club because, he said, it would get young people together with the excuse to play sports or to meet socially and then, afterward, on Fridays, they would be subjected to occult rabbinical interpretations of the Scriptures. For him, religion was the opiate of the masses, and, of course, Silvester didn't believe in crazy mediums or fortune-tellers either. Silvester used to say you can't predict the future because it doesn't exist; the future comes into being when you make decisions and then work to make it happen. And if Silvester ever refused to open an umbrella inside a house or say the word *death*, it was because of his good up-bringing.

By this stage of the game it's important to realize (and whatever The Book of Memories might say doesn't really matter because there are other sources, events, and documents that corroborate what happened) that Uncle Pucho's brother and sisters were quite worried, and his wife was desperate, Granny was mute, and The Indian Girl was dejected, which made you feel sorry for her, because three days had gone by and still no one knew where Uncle Pucho was. Gone was the snickering of the first night when they thought poor Pucho had simply gone out on the town, imagining him having a tryst in some whore's bed while he ate Russian salad.

They worried because the only thing they managed to do that first day of searching—the day they spent calling around and paying some visits—was eliminate the police stations and hospitals, his friends and past office cohorts and clients and suppliers. No one knew where he was. They even eliminated an ex-girlfriend and a friend of his first wife's and a certain young woman with green eyes who was an excellent pro and who Silvester had gone to see once without anyone ever knowing about it. All they hoped was that she had shared a Russian salad with Uncle Pucho at the Cavour Restaurant. The one with green eyes could have been with Uncle Pucho that night and other nights, but she wasn't. The second day they resorted to Silvester's method, which, like him, was organized and logical. First, they went through the clothing Uncle Pucho had been wearing recently and then drove around in Silvester's Buick with two other friends and their cars to look for that '49 Fiat, which was black on the outside and purple on the inside, that Uncle Pucho used mainly to drive to the soccer stadium.

The plan was methodically—Silvesterly—to comb the entire city. It wasn't necessary. They quickly spotted the Fiat because one fender had been shot up by a machine gun. In June of '55 it occurred to Pucho to invite his brother Silvester, wife, and kids to go out for a ride on the town. At the time everyone was happy because the Long-tailed Devil was about to die, but they got caught in the middle of some bomb explosions and cross fire, causing those holes in his fender; instead of getting them fixed immediately afterward, he left them to rust as a badge of courage.

Hence, it wasn't necessary to carry out the meticulous plan to comb the city as Silvester had decided to do the night before when he stayed up devising plans, mainly because he couldn't sleep. The first area they searched was around the Ferro Club and then they went to the movie area downtown. They quickly found the Fiat parked on Suipacha Street near the Ideal Coffee Shop. Silvester opened the door by using a metal coat hanger over the top of the window.

Inside the car, they found two movie tickets on the floor for "A Stranger Calls" with Bette Davis and Gary Merrill which was being shown at a nearby movie theater. The director of the film was Nunnally Johnson. One must remember that back then hardly anyone—much less the Rimetkas with their problem at the time—gave any importance to movie directors.

Uncle Silvester went to the theater where the movie was playing, but he couldn't find anyone who might have even vaguely remembered a balding, fat man accompanied by a young woman. Uncle Silvester had deduced that it was a woman because the only movies Pucho liked were war movies and some westerns; this wasn't the kind of movie to see with some male friend and, besides, there were two tickets. (Of course, they told Pucho's second wife that they found only one ticket, but she figured it out anyway because she knew that Pucho hated watching that hysterical, emaciated Bette Davis with eyes like two fried eggs, the truth being he would have gone only if someone had made him go, just like everything else he did in life, except when it came to watching a soccer match when Ferro was playing).

The car and the tickets were the only evidence they could muster using the methodical search method. Although they just went around in circles all day long, which was based on the information they had at hand, Silvester managed to make a few more observations: He deduced that Pucho was still alive, he hadn't left the city, and he was wearing enough warm clothing to be able to spend the night on the street. And he hadn't taken any money out of the bank.

His observations were more than good enough to win the game called Twenty Questions, but they weren't good enough to find Pucho. It was then Uncle Silvester gave up and said the same comforting words to Pucho's second wife that everyone who knew about it had been repeating clumsily for two days: let's stay calm, he's going to show up any moment now.

Those who knew about it were few in number, for once the possibility of an accident had been eliminated, Pucho's second wife became terribly embarrassed knowing that everyone might think he had run away (and without saying anything to anyone she promised herself that if he came back she was going to change completely their pattern of going out, eating meals, and other things). Hence, out of respect, the investigation, except for driving around in a car, was carried out discretely.

On the other hand, once the fear of tragedy had passed, Granny became openly and strangely happy, which was in direct opposition to the embarrassment that Pucho's second wife was experiencing. Like any other event in his life, Pucho's disappearance was yet another chapter in the long war he had waged against his wife and, for the time being, was managing to win.

And that's how, on that fateful third day, the Rimetka brother and sisters, including Silvester, ended up visiting Miss Blackie, a medium recommended by Aunt Clara. Everything smelled of incense; there had always been incense burners in the bathroom in the Old House which you could light to get rid of foul odors. That's why Judith and Silvester thought Miss Blackie's entire house smelled like a bathroom. It didn't bother Clara because she was already used to it. Pucho's second wife was in no condition to be thinking about odors.

Miss Blackie was a large woman, heavily daubed in makeup, and she attended to her clients seated at a table with a calypso tablecloth. On the table there was a metal ring sitting on a base with a crystal ball in the middle hanging from a wire. The crystal ball looked like it had been part of a chandelier, which it probably was.

The medium asked the brother and sisters and Pucho's second wife to look straight into the crystal ball which began to move, not because they were looking at it but because Miss Blackie had given a visible tug at the tablecloth. The ball started to go around in circles, while an obese fly buzzed around the window.

"I'm looking through his eyes, the eyes of the one you are seeking to find. I see . . . a small woman. Her facial features are strong, you can tell she's fierce, not a woman to play around with," Miss Blackie said, "she's wearing a fitted dress, and she's a blond. Her eyes . . . there's something about her eyes . . . like they're going to jump out of their sockets. . . ."

"It's Bette Davis," Clara screams excitedly.

When they were leaving afterward, Silvester made Clara swear on a stack of Bibles that she hadn't said anything to Miss Blackie about his investigation, the Fiat, and the movie tickets. Sobbing, Clara swore she hadn't.

Aunt Clara said that when they made her swear, she cried not because she was lying, for how could she lie at a time like this—her brother's life could very well be at stake—but because Silvester didn't believe her. And he not only didn't believe her but he also didn't believe Miss Blackie either, and she realized that if they didn't believe her, they were never going to find Pucho.

"Someone here loves him and someone else doesn't love him," Miss Blackie said. "It's like a negative magnetic field, and it's very close by, it's here in this room."

Miss Blackie peered into everyone's eyes.

"Everyone take a deep look inside themselves. Someone loves him, someone doesn't. Whoever doesn't love him, that person should leave now, 'cause I don't have the strength to deal with you."

It seemed like she had been doing battle with someone or something for quite some time. Her eyes were closed and she seemed to be struggling; she was tense and her face was covered in sweat. Adding the smell of incense, she looked like she was constipated.

So they looked deep inside themselves and then furtively to each side, as if they were waiting for her to trick them, and they all turned inward and saw how much they loved Pucho—or didn't love Pucho.

And Aunt Judith remembered that famous goal she scored against poor Pucho when she was playing for the Bacacay Juniors and also the time when Pucho gave her that little figurine from the box of Aguila Chocolates because he wanted to.

And the others also remembered the good things and the bad things, except for Uncle Silvester, who was trying to calculate how many stories about their family Aunt Clara had probably told that devious hussy, the medium. And, of course, no one was going to be that courageous—or stupid—to leave the room, especially in front of everyone else.

Then Miss Blackie asked them to leave her alone with the man's wife; afterward Pucho's second wife said that the woman knew everything about her husband, from his preferences down to the brand of undershirts he wore. (But Judith and Silvester always thought that to guess Pucho's brand of undershirts was probably the easiest thing to do in the world because the whole family—even Grandfather Gedalia because he never looked a gift horse in the mouth—used the same Pelusita brand made by Judith's husband Ramón).

Then Miss Blackie asked them to bring a piece of her husband's clothing, preferably a pair of underwear that was preferably unwashed. Pucho's second wife became distraught because she didn't have any of his dirty underwear and if she had she wouldn't have wanted anyone to see it anyway. But Miss Blackie put her at ease by also saying it didn't matter if they were washed and ironed.

And suddenly the whole scene changed: it was as if Miss Blackie had actually reached the limits of her strength and was unable to continue sustaining the import of the spectacle.

This time her daubed face became distorted, she lost control, and she couldn't stop herself. Tears flowed down her cheeks. Miss Blackie put her arms on the table, buried her face, and made a gurgling sound while she cried. The anguish was so horrible that Pucho's second wife, now frightened, was about to either run out the door or pat the woman on the head.

Then Miss Blackie raised her eyes and looked at her defiantly, with animosity. She opened a drawer, took out a piece of paper, and handed it to Pucho's second wife. The paper indicated the results of a biopsy and it didn't take much knowledge of medicine to understand what the words *carcinoma* and *neoplastic cells* meant.

"Do you want me to give you a real prophesy?" Miss Blackie said, speaking with hatred, "I've got one fucking year left. And your jackass husband is going to reappear again at any time, with his tail between his legs, and you're going to continue living with him and your plump little daughter for the next umpteen years while, me, I'm going to be dead and riddled by worms."

And what she told her about her husband was more or less the same thing that every one had told her, but seeing how she had told her in such a terrible way and was all daubed up with thick, colored makeup, like Theda Bara used to wear, streaming down her face because of the tears, Pucho's second wife believed her through and through. *With his tail between his legs*, she had told her, and perhaps it was the way she put it that effectively calmed her down, so much so that for the first time in three nights she was able to sleep as sound as a baby. And indeed she was sound asleep when Pucho reappeared in the early morning hours. Without saying a word, his tail between his legs, he put on his striped pajamas and got into bed next to his second wife.

And the next morning he said he didn't know what had happened to him because he couldn't remember a thing.

(Even though it's true, Pucho's poor second wife didn't live umpteen years nor many more at all; in fact, her destiny was quite similar to Miss Blackie's and, not surprisingly, she remembered her and her prophesy when she received the results of her first biopsy. All of which clearly demonstrated that Miss Blackie was a lousy fortune-teller, Judith would say, or that you can't tell the future because, like Uncle Silvester said, it doesn't exist).

And Uncle Silvester said Pucho had considered running away but then he felt guilty.

And Aunt Judith used to say the poor jerk had simply taken a vacation.

And Aunt Clara used to say it wasn't necessary to say such foolish things when the important thing was to have him back home and get things back to normal.

And Pucho's second wife had said it was amnesia brought on by those diet pills—Dr. Gdansk's famous torpedoes.

And Pucho didn't say a thing. After that incident, he didn't have to commit to a diet program either.

And the truth is Doctor Gdansk's torpedoes really produced weight loss but they also produced some strange side effects, like the time when Aunt Clara fainted in a drugstore and hit her head against the base of the weigh scales and knocked a hole in her skull.

And Lilian, Judith's daughter, turned completely yellow and they thought she had hepatitis, and she almost had to drop out of school for a year because of a strange chemical reaction.

And Uncle Yaco, Clara's husband, had some intestinal problems that confused the doctors and they almost diagnosed ulcerative colitis and he was a hair away from losing half of his intestines through surgery. It was a miracle they didn't operate on him.

And a friend of Silvester's became almost impotent.

And another friend of the family came down with diverticulosis.

And everybody was taking Dr. Gdansk's terrible torpedoes, the same ones that Uncle Pucho had been taking until the day he got lost, disappeared, ran away, or suffered from amnesia from those diet pills.

Time of Fear

The Book of Memories is our only legitimate source. That's why it can make you so mad: even though what it tells you is true, it never tells you everything, it simply doesn't provide all the information.

At times, people lie, distort, or exaggerate things and give their own version; that is, they interpret. But The Book of Memories limits itself to providing only the facts as they happened; it's as if they were happening that way at the moment we consult it. It also contains original documents whose authenticity is verifiable.

However, it so happens that we'd like to know, for instance, why Uncle Silvester got into a big fight with a government bureaucrat for which he was sent to jail and then faced trial because he beat up the guy so badly. And when we open The Book of Memories all we find is a picture of Uncle Silvester with a scar over his right eyebrow, or something like the color of the socks he was wearing that day. While this information is most likely correct, it's not what we need to re-construct what really happened. It's irritating.

For instance, in order to understand what happened between Aunt Judith and her daughter the day Uncle Ramón died, we would need information about not only the period preceding the military dicta-torship but also the period of the 1976–83 dictatorship itself. How-ever, the only thing we find in The Book of Memories is a literary text, poorly written in longhand by some third-generation Rimetka family member on paper without lines with a blue pen. While from one perspective the text itself is authentic, the information it con-tains isn't.

In reality, when all is said and done, this document is just fictional literature and not an example of investigative reporting or a testi-mony about the times when the events take place. Its relationship to the facts is indirect; you could almost say the author uses them ad hoc, mixing them with invention and certain conventional literary tricks. It's not anything like a historical text. (Even though at times a short story or a novel can help to understand or to imagine more easily a period in time than a list of names and dates that ends up for-gotten or confused with the truth of what happened to the people involved.)

Another initial clarification, made with a ball-point pen of a dif-ferent color, shows that the person who's telling the story wanted to write about the Time of Fear, something that would show people who had never experienced that time period what happened in that coun-try, what it was really like.

When the writer began to think about how to narrate some of the stories, he or she realized that there were many books that already dealt with the topic. And, above all, there isn't any piece of fiction on the subject that could be as good, interesting, or important as the testimonies of those who had survived the ordeal.

Finally, when he or she began to write, the most interesting part wasn't what had happened, because it was being told in great detail and had already attained the image of truth, but rather what the people knew and had learned about it, because some of them had suffered through it, others because they had heard about it, and everyone because they feared it. These fragmentary bits of information weren't everything, but they were enough to create a great deal of fear, more than enough, in fact, so that this era could be called just that: the Time of Fear. And anyone who has experienced it would know what we're talking about.

Time of Fear

One can also experience fear on a roller coaster ride but that's different; in that situation, it's a strong, jabbing fear, like the sensation of turning a glove inside out, only it's your stomach. Driven to escape but unable to, the quick fright is right there, and afterward, if you want, you can try it again, and you know it's there waiting for you.

But when the fear is strong and never-ending, you stop feeling it, it becomes a part of your flesh and fat, it travels through your veins and makes a home in the liver and then people begin to forget about it, they just go about filling themselves up with that sticky fear, a fear that erupts any time, believing they live and sleep as usual, although now it's more dense, slower, defining each gesture.

It's hard to explain the Time of Fear to those who didn't experience it. It was never-ending. Everyone became so accustomed to living with fear that many weren't even aware they were afraid anymore.

It's impossible, for example, to compare the fear people have who live in New York, where there is so much violence. There, according to what people say, you find some straightforward rules to follow: it's not wise to go out late at night, there are areas everyone knows are off limits, a white person shouldn't venture into Harlem, and taxis are a safe haven. It's true anyone can become involved in a chance incident, your house could be broken into or you could be robbed on the subway, but if you rigorously follow certain rules the probability of becoming a victim is less.

There have been those who have compared it with AIDS and it makes sense if you think of it as a type of epidemic, like a plague that lasts a long time. The big difference is that we know how AIDS infects a person, but during the period when people became blacklisted it was totally impossible to know (one could suspect, of course: the impossible was the only sure thing) how or by what means someone had become contaminated with the virus that blacklisted them.

And, above all, it was difficult to know ahead of time; in fact, discovering preventive measures made it all the more confusing and complicated: in general, they would come and take someone away. Afterward their names would appear on a list in some government office and that would be it.

Some of those who had been blacklisted did return home, though there weren't many of them. But then people looked at them with suspicion because they didn't say anything and it was difficult to know if they were still human beings. The truth is that the ones who returned would never look you straight in the eye; instead, they had a strange way of looking away that made us distrustful.

The truth is that when they took someone away who had been blacklisted, the feeling of danger became even stronger for those who knew the person because the next one could be the father or brother, even a fellow worker or one's lover or a friend with whom the disappeared person played tennis on Sundays.

There were many cases in which it seemed like the person who had been returned made everyone around him or her immune, that is, their friends and relatives never had problems again, but there were other cases in which entire families were taken away. And so it turns out that the lack of clear rules with respect to who might be blacklisted became the source of this special kind of fear. Some insisted that one should only drink mineral water and those who made soup or coffee with tap water became responsible for whatever might happen to them. Others used to say that only certain kinds of books and music should be read or heard. The editor of a writer who was publishing his first book of short stories was required to remove any bad words. The only word the writer found was *whore* and he took it out; instead of *whore* he put *woman* and it must have been acceptable because the book was eventually published.

And there were those who insisted there was no need to be fearful because that made it even worse. They compared it to what happens to a person who is afraid of dogs. They see a dog and take off running and the dog chases them out of pure instinct. And it's true dogs can smell fear in one's perspiration, adrenaline, or whatever, and they pounce on you. So, if someone goes around looking afraid, that alone seemed to be enough to be taken away. Whoever shows a sign of fear, the thinking goes, must have done something wrong.

But it was also important, they would say, to adhere to a dress code. People suggested, for instance, that women shouldn't smoke Turkish cigarettes and it shouldn't even occur to men to wear an earring. They advised against wearing loud colors: men could wear black, grey, or brown, and blue in some cases (since the men in this country have never liked wearing loud colors, this restriction wasn't much of a problem); and they advised women to wear pastel colors and combinations of jackets and skirts in tones of beige. That's the way it was if you gave credence to the people who believed that one becomes branded by what they wear.

Transmitting news by means of rumor was typical during the Time of Fear. News was something no one talked about openly, much less in public places. But every once in a while a friend would stop by your house for a cup of coffee and, in a muted voice, he or she would tell you the most unbelievable stories, like the ones about how they were making the blacklisted work in an underground storage area for nuclear waste or they would take them on a plane or in a helicopter and throw them into the ocean or how they would cut them up into little pieces and export them to England as corned beef. That's crazy! The ones who believed those stories did not waver. For example, if someone would try to explain to them that it would be cost-prohibitive to spend all that money on airplane fuel just to throw people into the ocean and that it was also a bothersome, dangerous, and uneconomic way to get rid of prisoners, they would say over and over again that we're not Germans here. That stock phrase also underscored the idea of our creativity and individuality, but also our disorganization, lack of a sense of practicality, and our inefficiency, all of which make our nation different from the more organized ones.

In a butcher shop one time, I saw a side of beef hanging from a giant hook. Blood was dripping onto the white marble floor. It just kept dripping and soon a small pool had formed. There were three men in the shop. It's not strange to see men in a butcher shop. Since men are the ones responsible to make a good beef barbecue, they are the ones who choose the cuts and the sausages themselves. But this time it was strange to see three of them together, all wearing suits and ties. One of them looked at the meat dripping with blood and laughed. I knew that guy, he laughed, and look how he ended up. The other clients in the store laughed along with him, just in case.

More information was being published outside the country than inside, and one could be led to believe that it was better, more reliable. But the people who came from other countries were confused by it all, they didn't understand what was happening: they believed, for instance, you might be in danger if you went skiing in Bariloche or went out at night. Those of us who were living in the country at the time just laughed at those ridiculous fears, but we couldn't deny them either.

There were blacklisted people who never disappeared forever; from time to time they would call on the telephone and talk to their families. They would say stupid things about the weather and, above all, they insisted they were just fine. They would deliberately mention the names of certain people who, once alerted, made speedy efforts to leave the country.

Many of those who had talked with their families by phone over weeks and months suddenly stopped calling without anyone knowing why. In some cases, the families knew where they were, at least for a time, and one could walk down the street knowing that in some part of a building nearby, one which you wanted to view with an X-ray machine, there was a friend locked up inside.

Some of the blacklisted would reappear at home on Mother's Day, for example, and then they would leave again, only this time who knows where.

Nevertheless, there was always someone who was luckier than the rest because on the day they would go looking for him he wouldn't be at work or he might be at someone else's house, and the doorman, a family member, or an office worker would warn them. And if they had their passport in order, they could attempt to leave ahead of time.

And it's true there were people who were smuggled away at the airport; once a plane was stopped from taking off in order to remove a woman and her children. Those were isolated cases, but it was one of the few ways one could escape.

And there were people who were unaware of what was happening or they were too poor to go to another country, or the only thing they could do is move to another neighborhood and, perhaps, save themselves.

There's a smudged page here, making it almost illegible. Then the text stops altogether. But we shouldn't complain: it's rare to find so much information about a topic in The Book of Memories, even if it is ridiculous, false, or exaggerated.

It's important to point out that if the blacklisted people mentioned in the book seem a little like the "missing" in Argentina, there's no way you can create a simple parallel between the two situations. In general, the people who were really missing were not chosen arbitrarily; in general there was some reason that was related to politics, even though the motives might involve a member of someone's family, or a friend, or someone who was under suspicion. And mistakes were made, of course, and there was some question involving economic and personal revenge, but in no way could you say they were the majority. But, no matter how you look at it, this text meets the purpose for which it was intended: to give an idea of the situation at the time the events described in the next chapter did occur.

Selva or Lilian:
Aunt Judith's Daughter

At the casino when it's time for everyone to place their bets, some people play the numbers that appear more frequently, while others play the less frequent ones. When an airline breaks a record for accident-free flights, the people responsible (and, above all, those responsible for the publicity) prefer that no one finds out. Because not many people are really disposed to think that the airplanes of that company are maintained any better or worse than the airplanes of other airlines, or that their pilots are better or worse. The disbelievers will always say they've just been lucky so far, and just when you go for the pot, you lose it all. And even those who play it out normally are going to say it's not good to abuse a winning streak. And, for that matter, why remind people that airplanes do crash anyway?

Because even those who don't believe in destiny, like Uncle Silvester, do believe in winning streaks: there are good times and lean times. It's just that no one knows how long they will last.

But when Aunt Judith's daughter died the way she did, everyone thought her streak of bad luck had been too long and too severe.

There's an ink drawing of Aunt Judith's daughter in The Book of Memories, probably to remind everyone that she was dark, with hair almost as black as The Indian Girl's, although her skin was somewhat lighter, or maybe just a different hue, more olive-colored than copper-colored. She had extremely long, straight hair and she didn't smoke those dark cigarettes (she liked Players with filters and the strong Parisian brands) because they had advised militant women to smoke the lighter brands in order to conceal their identities.

The name *Selva* was printed underneath the drawing in capital letters. Actually, Selva wasn't called Selva but rather Lilian, but she would have preferred that everyone remember her as Selva, with such long hair (a little bit longer than she had in reality) and the name that she herself (not her mother or father) had chosen.

But even in The Book of Memories you can't rely on everything as truth: there are those who say (even though this sacrilegious theory has never been proven) that at times The Book remembers things that never happened; at times its memory softens and takes a rest.

It's not that the girl wasn't in danger; to the contrary, if Lilian (or Selva) had died because of what the statistics of the World Health Organization indicate as the principal cause of death among young people in this country during that time, no one would have blamed it on bad luck. It was quite easy for someone her age and in her situation to die during the Time of Fear (although Lilian didn't die because she was an activist). That S.O.B. upstairs, Aunt Judith would say, punished me by giving me a Peronist daughter. And she would raise her eyes to the sky in consternation (although her daughter didn't die because she was a Peronist follower either).

A drunken father and a foul-mouthed mother, Uncle Pucho would say, what could you expect of her? But he only spoke like that before Lilian died, before, in fact, Uncle Ramón's death, and before, above all, becoming aware that The Indian Girl, so timid and quiet, had fallen under the spell of the Long-tailed Devil who—now old, weak, and a bully—was trying to fill his ranks with the children of his old ex-enemies.

(The Crazy-Lady-Around-the-Corner, the poor thing, or maybe lady luck had smiled on her just the same, had died before seeing the face of the Long-tailed Devil on TV again or before finding out, poor thing, about the death of her Angel Aramburu at the hands of young Peronists.)

And Aunt Clara, speaking with the authority of her son's words, who by then had finished studying to be a psychologist, which is even worse, used to say that the problem with her niece Lilian was that she had something against the family, it was her rebellious nature, a defense mechanism, she'd say, against her mother who was so authoritarian but didn't know how to put limits on things. And she remembered when they were small children and Aunt Judith, who was her older sister, would drive her crazy over nothing.

The one who seemed to be in less danger was Aunt Judith's husband, with his baggy pants because of his shrunken waistline and his little undergarment factory (using the interlock patent) that the entire Rimetka family wore up through the third generation until they began to rebel against family ways). Nevertheless, it was Uncle Ramón who died first.

For all the little cousins, to go to Aunt Judith's house meant going to a party because in the garage, where the shop was set up, there were piles and piles of scraps of different types of cloth that were perfect for making not only dolls' clothes but also other things that weren't easy to imagine unless you were there. For example, when one of Silvester's children, the one who was obsessed with animals, built a birdcage, he used pieces of interlock cloth for the birds to make their nests. The young pigeons were raised very comfortably in their nests of unravelings and strips of cloth, soft and smooth, and hardly hygienic.

Aunt Judith's husband made underwear—panties, shorts, t-shirts, and sleeveless undershirts—all with high-quality cloth. He was healthy, drank whiskey, and told dirty jokes; nevertheless, he died before anyone else, before Grandfather Gedalia, for example, which was against the laws of nature, Silvester used to say. He believed in the laws of nature, the same laws, of course, that would respond with absolute indifference, unheedingly, to his display of confidence, and, in general, treating him as arbitrarily as the laws of men. And Uncle Ramón died before his daughter Selva (or Lilian), even though it's not that rare, but it's something that all parents hope for: to die before their children.

Now my generation's next, Grandfather Gedalia used to say, but I'm not ready to go just yet. They hadn't started to come for Aunt Judith's husband, but he went just the same. It was simple: he had a heart attack in the hospital after a lousy gall bladder operation.

Uncle Silvester says it was more than just a gall bladder operation or, at least, it wasn't just a gall bladder operation. He says Aunt Judith's husband had cancer and they wanted to keep it a secret from the children, but to keep something a secret from the children never works.

Aunt Judith says why the hell would they want to keep it a secret when he ended up dying anyway. He had gallstones and that's that. And she even has a little wooden box with a little pile of blackened sand inside—her husband's gallstones—in the event anyone wants proof.

Aunt Clara says no one knows her sister like she does, that's why she's her sister's only sister, and Uncle Silvester always behaves as if he were God, telling everyone what's right and wrong, and what Aunt

Judith's husband had were huge hemorrhoids as big as cucumbers that Aunt Judith, foul-mouthed and everything that she is, was embarrassed to admit.

It had to be Clara, Aunt Judith says, my screwed-up sister Clara, who would be the one to stick her nose up a dead person's ass: a poor stupid dead body about which they can say whatever they want because he's not there or in any condition to defend his own ass, meaning she neither confirmed nor denied her sister's declarations.

There's a detailed description in The Book of Memories of what happened in the hospital room (that was taken from a version Lilian or Selva got from some of their friends) after Uncle Ramón turned blue and died, but it doesn't say anything about why he died or had ended up that way.

Uncle Ramón turned blue and died and then began to take on that cream-colored texture so typical of dead people, and it was strange because his cheeks and nose were always red with lots of little veins running through them. That color is so difficult to describe because there's no word anyone can agree on: they usually say "natural" when one talks about cloth, "cream-colored" about a wall or some other object, and "waxen" about someone's face, even though one could imagine the face of a dead person as an object, too.

Aunt Judith was with him in the room when everything happened; afterward, Lilian said it was luck she was there because her mother could be assured of having done all that she could for him—everything she could and couldn't do for him—because if she would've been there replacing her mother at that moment, Lilian thought, then her mother would have never forgiven her.

Forgive who?

She would have never forgiven herself.

Oh, I see. I thought you meant Lilian.

She wouldn't have been able to forgive her either.

Now we're on track.

She would have pardoned her, but she never would have been one hundred percent sure that she did everything possible, absolutely everything, and everything impossible.

But one thing for sure is that the one who was with Uncle Ramón in the hospital room was she, his wife. And, hence, Aunt Judith herself was the one who had the opportunity to run out of the room screaming for the nurses, and she was present when they gave him the shots and a heart massage and brought the oxygen tent and the heart medicine and everything else. So there was no way she was going to be able to blame anyone else.

Afterward, when the remains of Uncle Ramón had turned cream-colored or waxen, Aunt Judith, who was at his side massaging his chest to keep it warm, asked a nurse nearby to call her children.

But the first ones to arrive weren't her children, they were some other people—an old man and his wife—who were there to visit the patient in the room next to Uncle Ramón's. Mistakenly entering his room, they didn't know how to leave because Aunt Judith talked and talked and said bad words and kept massaging the dead man's chest in order to keep it warm.

A nurse would come in from time to time and stroke her hair saying poor thing, poor thing, until Aunt Judith told her to fuck off and the nurse had to leave, but even as she walked down the hall she kept repeating poor thing. And Aunt Judith just kept on rubbing the cadaver's chest: she rubbed it to keep it warm.

The first of the children to arrive was Pochoclo. They hadn't informed him of anything on the phone and so he went to the bathroom first. Although he was suspicious when he arrived, it's something else to actually confirm the misfortune of having no options. One might guess he went into the bathroom to vomit but, in reality, it was because of a state of induced diarrhea: Pochoclo didn't have nerves of steel (his mother used to say it's better to shit your pants than to be shit on) and diarrhea and anguish were one and the same for him. While anyone else might have suffered from an asthma attack, a headache, or the violent tightening of one's neck muscles around the throat, for him it was always an urgent need to empty his bowels. Crying and choking from pain and sorrow, he leaves the bathroom and Aunt Judith immediately puts him on the other side of the bed to work with her, rubbing the cadaver's chest. They rubbed and rubbed to keep it warm.

It's amazing how the gossip spread so fast to so many people. And there's no agreement as to who was actually there. The only thing for certain is that when Aunt Clara arrived (perhaps before or after Lilian had to swear under oath) she wanted to faint but no one would let her.

What is certain is that when Lilian had to swear under oath to her mother and brother, there were many witnesses present, and since there were so many opinions about her taking an oath, it really wasn't necessary for a single witness to have been there.

Uncle Pucho used to say Aunt Judith was always so dramatic that she could turn anything into a big show, and even when it involved the most intimate or brutal circumstances, she acted as if there were five hundred spectators watching her. He'd also say you had to excuse the melodrama in this case because of the stress she was under.

Of course, Uncle Silvester thought it was all in bad taste. The others were saying he always defended his sister Judith, but why didn't he this time? And Uncle Silvester argued with Pochoclo who, in turn, tried to explain to him, to his Uncle Silvester, that this time he agreed with him, but nevertheless . . .

It was important for Pochoclo, Aunt Judith's youngest child, to impress his Uncle Silvester and demonstrate to him the type of person he was. It was an infinitely hard task, an exhausting task, because no one was ever good enough for Silvester, you had to keep showing him over and over. It was as if Silvester was always waiting for someone, almost to the point of secretly desiring that he try to pull a trick on him and, hence, demonstrate human frailty, perform some discrete exhibition of egotism or unfaithfulness or greed or some imperfection that would allow him to retract his sacred and fragile faith in human beings. Every man is innocent before the law as long as there's no contrary evidence, Silvester would dictate, and in everyday life, like everyone knew who was close to him, he was always predisposed to think the worst of everyone. He was always ready to call someone guilty until proven innocent.

So Pochoclo tried to demonstrate just the opposite and explain to his Uncle Silvester why his mother had done what she did (rubbing the cadaver's chest, rubbing hard to keep it warm) because of that unexplainable sensation one feels when someone close to you dies, that sensation of complete helplessness, that sensation when you realize any person and, specifically, you yourself and the persons you love, could die at any moment, just like that. It's something that's true but it's something people forget in order to distract themselves from reality. Because Pochoclo thought if he could make Silvester understand (but no one who had experienced this situation could believe him), he would realize that Aunt Judith wasn't so reprehensible; however, what's reprehensible is when someone you love dies, after which just about everything else becomes meaningless.

In time, Lilian began to talk about what had happened in that hospital room. She described it to her militant friends (the ones who called her Selva), but not to everyone, only to those whom she thought would understand (the ones who had known her from before and knew that she was also called Lilian).

She began explaining to them that when she got to the hospital room, her mother and brother were rubbing his chest, they were rubbing hard to keep it warm. And her mother, Aunt Judith, said come here, touch your Dad's chest, we were still rubbing it, Pochoclo and

I, trying to keep it warm, so that you could touch it while it was still warm, so that you could say goodbye to your Dad while his chest was still warm.

And Lilian didn't want to touch the chest of a dead person, who had his new pajamas on, the light summery type, and whose chest was hairy and skin a light cream color which wasn't like him but rather like a dead person who fit perfectly into the surroundings. But Aunt Judith took her by the hand and forced her to put it on the cadaver's chest that was truly warm, not on the inside but on the outside, the warmth coming from his wife's and younger son's hands who had been rubbing ever so vigorously.

And now, she told her, with her hand on her father's chest, I want you to swear on your father's warm chest that you'll stop being an activist. I want you to swear to me that never, ever will you go back to those fucking party headquarters.

But Lilian knew that the majority of her comrades was going to think it was ridiculous or exasperating or cowardly to have to swear an oath like that, but it would be even more ridiculous if she obeyed it. Hence, she carefully chose to whom she would tell the story and forgot about the rest of them. And, then, little by little she stopped going to the meetings, letting them think whatever they wanted: that she had given up or, out of fear, that she just couldn't take it anymore. And Selva's comrades, the ones who didn't know her real name (Lilian) or anything else about her, because that's the way they had to treat each other, compartmentalized, believed just that: she had given up, couldn't take it anymore, which was a common phenomenon those days. They were entering the initial phases of the Time of Fear and if, on the one hand, there was no sense of vocation, there was on the other the feeling that those who stayed in were going to rise rapidly to better, but more dangerous positions, positions vacated by others who couldn't make it or just gave up, ending their futures.

Hence, after taking the oath Lilian abandoned her activist ways or at least she stopped going to those fucking party headquarters which was in reality the only thing she swore to her mother she would do.

And she managed to deceive Aunt Judith, for a time anyway.

But she couldn't deceive The Book of Memories because it's much more difficult to deceive. If at times The Book of Memories doesn't say the full truth, it's because it doesn't want to, not because it doesn't know the truth. And in The Book of Memories it states that Lilian immediately became an activist again in the Peronist University Youth Brigade and, since she was hard-working and serious, in a matter of months she was occupying more important political positions and had represented the party on an academic board at the university.

But when she died, barely two years after Uncle Ramón, it wasn't because of her activism (even though due to the level of activism at the time, many people died that way).

An Appendix Revealing How Little Is Known
About Lilian's (or Selva's) Death

One day Selva didn't call her contact person. That day her contact was a redheaded girl who was always agitated and never left her house without her swoosh swoosh: that's what she called her aerosol medication that asthmatics get high on in order to breathe easier.

They advised or probably demanded that the girls in the Long-tailed-Devil's University Youth Brigade wear skirts instead of pants, not smoke or only smoke regular light tobacco, and not call attention to themselves. All of which was impossible for the redhead: she was conspicuous and stood out everywhere with that combination of the red color and the wild curls of her Afro-style hairdo (even though permanents were in style again, the redhead's curls were natural, out of control), making it difficult to comb.

Selva was supposed to call Ruby to tell her everything was fine. Times were difficult. Group meetings and reunions never consisted of more than four or five persons, all of whom, supposedly, didn't know anything about each other. Everyone used a code name. In reality, they were old friends from college, they had studied together, and they had looked for each other on the registration rosters, so it was difficult to operate in secret and use one nickname but not another.

One thing for certain was that one day Selva didn't call her contact, neither when she was supposed to nor later. (Those were the times when the telephones in Buenos Aires worked tolerably well and no one could blame the silence on technical difficulties.) Once the amount of time they had established for security reasons had passed, the redhead who was the contact person began calling the others.

Immediately, Selva's comrades took on clandestine lives; that is, they left their homes to sleep at their grandparents' or uncles' houses, or with friends who were also more or less committed to the cause and would take them in, help them get situated, all the while displaying fear in their smiles and a feeling of compassion and irritation. At that stage of the game, all of them would have preferred to fly away or escape, but only if their comrades wouldn't find out, or if their own conscience wouldn't get in the way. Having to go out at night through the streets carrying a mattress from one house to another produced a blood-curdling, cold sweat. Until they would hear something about Lilian, excuse me, I meant to say Selva, no one could go home to sleep and, above all, go back to school.

Someone in the group, probably the redhead, who had also been Selva's classmate in high school, had been nice enough not to forget her real name or telephone number and, using a pay phone, called her mother to warn her.

Lilian, or Selva, was living alone in an apartment on Almagro Street. By the time Aunt Judith received the call, several days had passed since she had heard from her daughter.

You're a walking dead person. I prefer to cry for you as a dead person, Aunt Judith had said, before I find out you've been living in danger all this time. As if it weren't enough to have a Marxist ulcer in your brain, you have to have the Long-tail's diarrhea: what a cocktail.

And, thus, Aunt Judith found herself doing just what she had sworn to herself that she wouldn't do, ever, to one of her children, the same thing her father—Grandfather Gedalia—had done to her: lament her death while she's still alive. But life is mysterious and our destinies are enigmatic; no one can predict the future except God or fate or the forces of nature or the composition of your own DNA, someone had written with authority.

And, hence, as her father had lamented her death in life, Aunt Judith did the same with her daughter. But it wasn't the same, it wasn't the real thing, she didn't think it would be that way ever: she only acted like she was lamenting her death, she only pretended to be crying. For a few days, she harbored the secret but absurd hope that Lilian-Selva would choose her mother, the serenity of her mother, instead of those political principles. And she didn't think (or she did think but even then she still had hope) it wasn't possible to make a choice, opt for her mother or her mother's serenity when she's so young, when she's in that brief interval of life in which a person has the luxury of feeling responsible for him or herself, for his or her own body.

And so the redhead called Aunt Judith and told her no one had heard from Lilian.

Judith went to the building where her daughter was living. No one answered the doorbell. There was no indication that the door had been forced. She didn't have any keys.

Aunt Judith rang a neighbor's doorbell. She was an older lady whom Lilian had mentioned off and on. She would lend her an egg in an emergency and had a spare key in the event Lilian forgot hers (she had an unfair and prejudiced hatred for doormen).

The neighbor was about the same age as Judith. She was warm and friendly. She invited Judith in for a cup of coffee but Judith was too distraught to wait. The lady complained about the doorman and the condition of the building. They've had water problems for two days. The water tank went low and there was hardly any pressure left.

Lilian's apartment had her look about it: clean and orderly. They immediately heard a noise in the shower. That's why she didn't hear the doorbell, they surmised without saying a word. They knocked on the door of the bathroom but Lilian didn't answer.

Now they would have to call the doorman. Reluctantly, the man came up to the apartment but he couldn't open the bathroom door because it was locked from the inside. He went to look for his tools. In order not to break the door down, he took it off the hinges.

Lilian was in the tub. She wasn't Selva anymore. She was naked and dead, and the water from the shower was pouring over her body. At first, Aunt Judith was embarrassed that the doorman would see her daughter naked.

Afterward, she thought how happy her comrades would be to know she hadn't been taken away. They could return home, go back to school, and sleep in relative peace.

Several hours later, after she had called Pochoclo, her brothers, and sister and had done the paperwork to get the body out of the morgue, she had recuperated enough to feel anything. An unfortunate blow to the head, Lilian must have fainted and slipped, the autopsy said.

Two months later, the redhead who was Selva's contact died of an asthma attack while being tortured, but Judith and Pochoclo, who knew her, didn't find out until many years later.

And there's nothing else in The Book of Memories about the Time of Fear, a sad time.

About the Old House
and Its Many Fates

The Old House was decorated in an antiquated false French style. When Silvester got married it was remodeled from top to bottom in a modern false French style.

You meant to say for Clara's wedding.

Silvester's.

No, Clara's.

It was remodeled from top to bottom in modern false French for both of their weddings.

Did they change Louis the French king's number on the chairs?

Don't even bother to ask if they changed the numbers because no one ever knew, neither before nor after, and if anyone ever did know they don't remember. Instead of wallpaper, the modern French style consisted of painted designs on the walls in the Main Dining Room and the Vestibule.

What's a Vestibule?

It's part of . . . I don't know how to explain it.

How do you describe a Vestibule to such a young person who is only attuned to supermarkets and who doesn't even know what a grocery store is? Suppose that the staircase from the entrance downstairs comes to here and then it opens up to one side and then the other side. When you get to the top of the staircase you're in the Vestibule and it's round and you can run around it. It's good for playing tag and cops and robbers, and it's good for playing soccer on rainy days, but it's bad for religious paintings, hand-painted porcelain plates, and really bad for little Art Nouveau figurines and those imitation Chinese vases. But that's where they put it all. That's the way the Vestibule was in the Old House.

And what else did the house have?

There were lots of things. There was a Main Dining Room and a Small Dining Room and a Piano Room. And the Grandparents' Chamber, the First Chamber, the Middle Chamber, and the End Chamber.

You don't say chamber, you say room.

The End Chamber was the End Chamber. You're not going to call it the End Room. After being married ten years, Silvester and The Dumb Turk took a trip to Europe. Upon their return, they said one can take more advantage of and enjoy a trip when you have a good guide. And in the Sistine Chapel they had a German guide who didn't speak Spanish very well and translated everything literally, saying Final Justice for Last Judgment.

Which is like saying End Room instead of End Chamber. When Pucho married Martita they lived in the End Chamber, but when he married his second wife, they lived in the Middle Chamber.

There was also the kitchen, the pantry, the terrace and the patio, and the Terrace Chamber, and more Chambers.

And all of that, where was it?

It was where it's supposed to be: everything in its place. It's hard to explain, I can't even draw it.

The Debacle began after Silvester got married.

You mean to say after Clara got married.

The Debacle began after Silvester's wedding and after Clara's wedding, it wasn't a sudden and noisy rout but rather a slow disaster, even though many people place its beginning at the time when Grandfather Gedalia got out of the cloth business, that is, when Pucho was about to ruin the family with his fiber glass business.

The Debacle became visibly striking when the elegant ladies with the false goblets, and the accompanying lithe gazelles and the large leaves of the false vines around the false goblets began to flake off or deteriorate to the point that they had to stop the little kids from peeling them off; they had to stop them, because it was tempting, it even became an obsession, to peel them off like one peels a hard-boiled egg.

Pucho's adopted daughter, The Indian Girl, went to the Fine Arts Department where she landed not only the position of drawing professor but also a boyfriend. And since the two of them were in Fine Arts, they felt sorry for the poor ladies and the fallen gazelles (by then there wasn't much more than a shadow and a memory), and they offered to repaint the goblets. They didn't use a false goblet color, but rather a false Van Gogh with purulent greens and vibrating yellows. And on top of it all, since they didn't have any talent for it (but no one knew that) and they didn't even try to be good artisans (because they believed they had the necessary talent), they painted them badly, very badly, deplorably bad.

Aunt Clara thought everything turned out ugly and depressing and she began to cry, but almost no one ever saw her. (By then, she lived in the large apartment on Alvear Avenue.)

Uncle Pucho thought everything turned out really pretty, because anything his daughter did was just great.

Uncle Silvester thought it was ugly but at least it had much more detail.

Aunt Judith thought it looked like some kind of tuberculin vomit, but she kept her mouth shut because if she said anything they would tell her to put up some money to pay professional painters. This occurred after the Collapse that Grandfather Gedalia survived, when they applied hot and cold presses, the same time when Aunt Judith moved back to the Old House.

There used to be beautiful stained-glass windows in the Old House, with yellow and violet flowers around the frames, but little by little they got broken. At first, when a piece of stained glass was broken they'd just leave it that way, broken. Whenever a large piece got broken, they replaced it with polished glass. During the era when Grandfather Gedalia was ostentatious, they didn't have maids but servants and, later on, it was called a service staff. The service staff slept in the servants' quarters which were located on a mid-level floor that you entered halfway up the stairway leading to the back part of the house. The service staff consisted, for example, of the butler Josafat, who began as a servant. The one who began as a servant, became a maid, and went on to become a cleaning woman, after she had gotten old, was Blanca Argentina, whom Granny loved very much.

What about Elvira?

Elvira started out as a maid.

When Grandfather Gedalia became a miser, only the most loyal of the service staff stayed on.

Only the stupidest.

Only the best.

Only the worst.

The ones who couldn't get work anywhere else.

The ones who cared about us the most.

No one from that era, the early era, was left.

What do you mean? Didn't you just say that Blanca Argentina stayed on?

No, I'm mistaken. Back then the service staff were white and quite sophisticated because they came from Europe.

The Spanish women from Galicia weren't very refined.

The Italian women weren't very refined either.

They were as refined as anyone who came after them. Rural folk. Brown people. Mestizos. But they weren't really colored, with real dark skin. They were like . . . you know . . . like The Indian Gi . . .

You shouldn't say that.

OK. They were like Blanca Argentina then.

There was no basement in the Old House. Everything was on the second floor. The entrance on the ground level was narrow and there were businesses on either side: a grocery store and an umbrella store. If you were really skillful, you could dangle a fishing pole with a piece of bent wire on the end over the terrace in the back and steal bottles and other things from the storage area of the grocery store.

The two stores belonged to Grandfather Gedalia and at first the rent from them paid for a good part of the cost to keep the house going. But then the arbitrary and cruel Long-tailed Devil came along and froze the rents forever. And then the Rimetka family didn't earn a cent in rent. It was then the Rimetka family became poor and the grocery store and the umbrella store owners got rich.

Don't try to pull the wool over my eyes. Grandfather Gedalia always had a lot of money.

Grandfather Gedalia had money but he never spent it on the house or on his family or on anything in the world. Grandfather Gedalia had a lot of money circulating with which he made loans, and he had money stashed secretly in bank accounts overseas. Money shouldn't be spent, Grandfather Gedalia used to say, it should be invested. And so he invested money to make more money and that's the reason for the Debacle, the real Debacle, not poor Pucho's debacle with the fiber glass business and his postdated checks.

Then there was the Era of the Shopping Galleries. They were built everywhere and everyone wanted to go to the galleries. They bought all kinds of things in the galleries and everyone wanted to have businesses in the galleries. (The Era of the Shopping Malls came much later: just one sand castle after another.)

Desperate to take advantage of the abandoned property, the Rimetka brothers decided to put in a small gallery, with five or six stores, not counting the grocery and umbrella stores. The rents were still frozen but they managed to make a deal with the two store owners by offering them ownership of spaces at the entrance to the gallery.

Some (but they're not family) say they convinced Grandfather Gedalia that he could make a lot of money, arguing that he had nothing to lose.

Others (they're not family either) say they convinced Grandfather Gedalia he could make a lot of money selling or renting businesses in the gallery.

These were people who knew the family but didn't know Grandfather Gedalia.

The four siblings, who did know him well because he was their father, managed to convince Grandfather Gedalia only by collecting the money among themselves and paying him penny by penny the price of the property.

Pucho's second wife was excited with her husband's new business venture because he had failed in so many others. But Uncle Yaco, Clara's husband, and The Dumb Turk, Silvester's wife, who were the only ones doing well in the family, didn't really want to put money into the new gallery.

The Rimetkas put up the land and the construction company put up the rest.

The construction company belonged to The Ottoman, The Dumb Turk's father. When The Ottoman got involved, The Dumb Turk stopped opposing the venture.

The gallery was built. Without putting up a red cent, the umbrella and grocery store owners got the choicest locations.

After the siblings sold the other locations and settled up their account with the builder, each one of the four brothers and sisters received the same amount of money they had put up in order to buy the land from Grandfather Gedalia.

Pucho's wife was happy because it was one of a few business ventures in which her husband had lost no money.

Many nasty and derogatory things were said about The Ottoman and they didn't come just from Aunt Judith.

The Ottoman and The Dumb Turk offered to show anyone their ledgers and said the construction company lost money because the business spaces were sold on credit and, in the meantime, inflation had eaten up the money.

That's the way it is in Argentina. You lose money in just about any type of business there is.

Silvester defended his wife and father-in-law.

The Book of Memories also says that's the way it is in Argentina.

You don't need The Book of Memories to know that.

The gallery was narrow and ugly and had nothing attractive about it other than what the stores were selling in the windows. When the Era of the Galleries was over, the gallery in the Old House went under. The businesses facing the street managed to survive while inside the gallery not much remained: a locksmith's shop, a photocopier, an upholsterer who did house calls, and a house appliance repairman's shop. They were businesses that had nothing attractive to put in their store windows, and a gallery without decorated store windows is destined to die.

And a house without a front is also destined to die.

It couldn't have died if there was a family inside that cared about it and looked after it.

But it was a worthless piece of property, so it died anyway. Despite its large size, it wasn't suitable for building anything.

But of course it's good for building something.

I say it's not.

With the new building codes, you might be right. Before, though, it was.

Not even then. And you're trying to tell me something different?

What's certain is when Granny died and Grandfather Gedalia broke his hip and the house was put up for sale because they couldn't keep it up, they appraised it low. Very low.

So low that Pucho asked permission from his father and brother and sisters to try another business. The house became a kindergarten and then a dance saloon.

After Pucho ruined the kindergarten venture and the dance saloon went bust, the house was sold.

First it was a photographer's studio. They could take advantage of the high ceilings.

Then it became an English Institute.

Then it became a club for retired people.

But before it became a club for retired people, it was something else.

What else?

I'll tell you later in private because they're writing down everything we say.

For some reason no business ever did well in the Old House, even the businesses in which poor Pucho wasn't involved.

Before becoming a club for retired people, the Old House was the Tajmahal.

The Tajmahal?

The famous Tajmahal in the Flores neighborhood. That was in the Era of the Massage Parlors.

And why didn't they use the name *Kamasutra*, which would have been more appropriate?

Because Kamasutra was old-sounding, conventional, overused, fourth-rate, and the owners wanted to believe they were inaugurating a new era, a new level of prestige. That's why they chose Tajmahal, which is more refined.

Before it went under, the Tajmahal had its moment of glory. So much so that the owners bought out the storeowners in the gallery and tore it all down in order to expand. The Tajmahal put racket ball courts at the back in order to better serve its active clients.

That's the way it is in this country. The Era of the Galleries comes and everyone builds galleries. Then comes the Era of the Ice Skating Rinks and everyone builds ice skating rinks. Then comes the Era of Imported Goods and everyone starts selling imported goods. Then comes the Era of the Cookie Factories and everyone builds cookie factories. Then comes the Era of the Massage Parlors and everyone gets into massage parlors.

You say everyone but you're really talking about a well-to-do middle class. You say everyone as if the country stopped at Buenos Aires city borders. You're talking as if there were no slums, no unskilled labor, no one working in the fields, no immigrants from Bolivia or Paraguay, no poverty on the outskirts of the cities, where 30 percent live in poverty and 60 percent have no sewage systems or enough clean water.

I'm saying everyone, but don't be stupid. When I say everyone, you know perfectly well what I mean. You know which everyone I'm talking about.

You mean to say just anyone can come up with the idea of a massage parlor? Some businesses aren't for just anyone. There are businesses that take talent, you've got to be there tending to it all the time.

You've got to be there in any business. And I'm not saying just any business. You've got to know that type of business. There's the sauna, the attendants, the parlor itself.

And how come you know so much about it?

Ask your cousin Gastón, Clara's son. He's the one who knows everything. Then you'll find out what kind of clients fill his office. Then you'll find out what kind of specialty he is talking about at the psychology meetings. And while you're at it, if you're up to it, ask him what happened to Uncle Pucho and a friend of one of his clients, uh, sorry, patients. It was a friend, or an acquaintance, or a friend of a friend. I'm not sure how it goes, but I do know that it was talked about a lot in the social circles. In that type of social circles. And it takes every type.

Pucho Returns
to the Old House

They believe one fat and bald Uncle Pucho got to the front door of the Old House by midafternoon. In fact, it was three o'clock in the afternoon.

They believe (since no one can prove it) that was the exact time. And no one believes he was fat and bald, everyone really knew he was. He was also old and sad. He was wearing a suit and tie. His suit and tie were also old and sad. Threadbare.

He probably pressed the electric door opener and went slowly up the stairs, puffing all the while, stopping to rest halfway up. He probably noticed the door didn't have polished glass in it anymore but the marble staircase, like the polished banister, was still impressive looking. There's little doubt he didn't go up the stairs, but the rest is open to conjecture. And it's not a matter of a simple supposition that's impossible to prove, but rather a logical deduction that his brother Silvester could have made based on information he was told and given by witnesses.

Did Uncle Pucho remember that it was no less arduous for his own Uncle Samson, Granny's brother, to climb those stairs? Every Saturday afternoon, Uncle Samson would arrive huffing and puffing, worn out from all the work he had to do in order not to work. First of all, he had to walk block after block in order to celebrate Saturdays at his sister's house, because it is forbidden to travel by car on the Sabbath. He had to knock on the wrought-iron door with his umbrella handle because it was forbidden to ring the doorbell on Saturday. But now the Old House was the Tajmahal, the imposing, famous Tajmahal in Flores and there were no more celebrations on the Sabbath. Now there were celebrations everyday, with parties that Uncle Samson never would have condoned.

The girl said it happened in the afternoon. The concern about the time of day is important because this story was reconstructed based on witnesses who know only a part of what happened, and the coincidence of the hour is one of the facts that brings the two parts of the story together and makes it attributable to Uncle Pucho.

The girl who told the story about what happened in the Tajmahal was named Sandra or something like that (or Rosario, Monica, Susana, or Elizabeth), but Sandra was the name she used at work unless, that is, one of her clients would choose to call her by some other name.

And is it possible to know to whom she told the story? Does anyone know who it was?

Of course we know. We know everything. Sandra told it to Claudia, her best friend who worked at another place called the Jet Set.

The Jet Set on 11th Street?

No! The Jet Set in the Minicenter.

And Claudia was one of Gastón's patients.

No way! How could she be a patient? If it had been she, we wouldn't be mentioning her by name. The names of patients aren't mentioned because doctors aren't supposed to reveal them. They're not supposed to be mentioned or written down anywhere. Just the initials and three dots. That's why psychoanalysts' reports look like Russian novels.

Don't say psychoanalyst because it's not the same. To be a psychoanalyst is one thing, to be a psychologist is another. My doctor is a psychoanalyst and a member of APA. He also teaches. It's not the same thing.

Whoever has money does whatever he wants. But just so you'll know, Gastón is also a psychoanalyst. If what he does is psychoanalysis, then he's a psychoanalyst.

You really want to say psychotherapist. Like the gestaltists, the transactional analysts, the ones who do music therapy, psychodrama, counseling, alternative healing, you know, those types.

I mean the APBA Psychoanalysts Association that also has international recognition.

Perhaps.

Why "perhaps"? What's important here is the story the patient told.

It takes all types.

Aunt Clara says her son Gastón quickly became independent; he wasn't like some of those psychologist sons who spend years and years working for free in some hospital or not even that and have to be supported by their families because they barely make enough to cover their medical studies.

Silvester (who was always up with the times) says it doesn't make sense to chase after the pimps anymore because the laws prohibiting pimping made sense back when they used to abduct women and force them into prostitution against their will, like in Clara Beter's time. In reality, though, the whore-pimp relationship represents an indivisible sociological unit and it can't be seen in terms of good and bad: if they try to rehabilitate the whore, then they have to rehabilitate the pimp, who is no less marginal or rejected by society. That's what they say.

Aunt Judith's son Pochoclo (who, belonging to a later generation, is even more up-to-date) says it's no use trying to rehabilitate anyone; the only thing bad about being a whore is that you're held in bad repute, it's not the profession itself, which is nothing more than a type of service that has always been in demand in every society, culture, and civilization, and even in primitive tribes which are the noblest of all. If whores were to receive some form of social recognition, they would be the source of pride of their fathers and teachers.

Before, when Uncle Pucho talked about Aunt Judith's children—Pochoclo and Lilian—he used to say those two kids were too modern. Which is to say they were impertinent. Which is to say their mother hadn't raised them right. Which is to say their mother Aunt Judith was also too modern.

Aunt Judith says there's no reason to put anyone down, because being a psychologist for whores is a lot better than being a pianist in a whorehouse.

Aunt Clara's psychologist son, Gastón, tells the story about the first whore to show up in his office. It was by pure chance because he had been recommended by a cousin of hers who had gone to see him in the Children's Hospital about her asthmatic son. And due to friendships and conversations at work, one whore after another started recommending him. It got to the point that he suddenly realized he had established a new specialization and began reading papers at conferences on the topic.

The whores, who were loyal and paid on time, were good patients and very mindful of the psychoanalytic process because, in reality, it was similar to their own type of work and not unlike the rules by which they would attend to their clients (rules that they would like men to respect in the same way that they respect the rules imposed by Dr. Rimetka).

For reasons concerning their type of work (and, during certain times when inflation was rampant which made it more convenient), Gastón allowed them to pay per session instead of monthly. Before leaving his office, they would put the money in an envelope and leave it on his desk. Afterward, they would laugh among themselves, calling it "a little present," even though they would have never said that to the doctor himself because they would be setting themselves up for some kind of analysis.

Since when do they analyze whores?

What do you mean since when? We're in Buenos Aires. Don't you know that everything here, right down to the Obelisk, is analyzed.

Do they put the Obelisk on a couch?

No, they do it face to face.

Unlike his mother, Aunt Clara, who spent her life interpreting everything, pointing out things, and bugging people with different psychoanalytic obsessions, Gastón was a psychoanalyst with street smarts who preferred using gutter terminology instead of the language of his profession. Only when he's in his office, where he would use all the fancy terminology necessary to impress his patients, he used as much verbosity as necessary. He was a happy slob who differed from the other fat Rimetka family members in that he enjoyed life and food and had never, ever, gone on a diet. (Except for the time when he was ten years old and his mother had taken him to Dr. Gdansk for the torpedo prescription. After taking Dr. Gdansk's torpedoes for a month, Gastón had become so weak that he could hardly get out of bed. His parents had to carry him to the bathroom and the doctor diagnosed muscular atrophy for lack of potassium.)

When the first wave of imported cars hit the country, Gastón bought a cream-colored Subaru that he cared for lovingly. Expert thieves who specialized in certain replacement parts stripped it clean: one afternoon he went to get it out of the parking garage and all he found was a body and a motor. Gastón turned in a police report and a few days later an officer who was a friend of his called to say they had found the thief. However, since they had no evidence against him, they were going to let him go. In this type of democracy, the officer said, we can't come down hard on anyone. Frankly, we can't even function like that. Gastón arrived just in time to find the apparent thief walking down the street. He introduced himself in a friendly way and invited him for a cup of coffee.

Two hours later the guy took him to a shop filled with the stolen parts and agreed to resell to Gastón the entire interior of his beloved Subaru at a reasonable price, almost at cost. And if there was no way to recover the parts for free, the young thief who was intelligent and very timid, asked for a session for his phobic brother who later became an excellent patient, going four times a week and, most likely, forever.

Much of this has little to do with what happened to Uncle Pucho in the Tajmahal in Flores, but it does explain something about Gastón and how he found out about the incident in so much detail, much of which isn't necessarily true.

The patient who told him the story was M., who she said she had heard it straight from Claudia (of the Jet Set), who was Susana's (of the Tajmahal) very best friend.

Stretched out on the couch, M. sobbed as she spoke. Tears streamed into her ears. And she wasn't crying over the person in the story she was telling, but for herself due to a personal incident that this story evoked and to which it's not necessary to refer since it doesn't have anything to do with this story.

When Gastón heard her mention the Tajmahal, he immediately

abandoned his wayward attention (that is, those uncomfortable moments that allowed him to solve crossword puzzles or play his son's Tetris game while his patients were talking) and began asking very specific questions about that place.

M., who had personally never worked in the Tajmahal and had heard the story secondhand, wasn't able to answer many of his questions, but they didn't surprise her because for over a year now she's been in therapy and she was used to listening and responding to absurd matters involving the details of some dream, a real-life person, or her Aunt Veronica's house in Mar del Plata, where she used to spend her vacations when she was little.

This time, however, M. didn't realize that the doctor wasn't interested in those details for therapy purposes, but showed a pure, sudden, and strong curiosity to learn about the transformations that took place in the Old House, going as far back as the time when the entire family would get together on Saturdays at midday to eat mayonnaise that Granny had whipped herself.

For professional reasons—in order to avoid current, future, or potential patients, or friends of friends of friends—Dr. Gastón (who, in reality, only had a Master's degree) couldn't go to saunas, private clubs, or massage parlors, not even the Tajmahal. And he really wanted to know what happened, for example, to the Piano Room, or the fate of the Vestibule, what function the Last Room has now, the room where he read about Freud for the time in the series "Important Men and Women" and the Mexican magazines that his cousin The Indian Girl collected, traded, and sold. Back then, she was the only cousin living in the Old House.

But the only thing Gastón was able to discern from M.'s story was that they had bought and gutted the businesses in the back part of the gallery and had created a space for tennis and racket ball.

Next, M. began telling a story about which the good doctor had not the slightest personal interest: in a state of attentive daydreaming, he floated between the words of the patient and his own personal thoughts.

The girl said Claudia (of the Jet Set) had heard it from Sandra. Apparently, Sandra had been complaining about the outright tyranny of the new marketing director at the Tajmahal. It seemed like the man was trying to optimize their investment in all the company's businesses, which included two third-rate saunas and a chain of Class-B discotheques. This marketing director was going to impose an excessively rigid organizational plan at the Tajmahal.

And, hence, all the girls had to dress in uniform: silver-colored bikinis that didn't fit some of them because, well, you know, M. would say, the problem of bras is a personal thing and no two breasts are the same and the bikini style may fit one person but it might not work for someone else. And they had to wear them while they were on duty, attending to a client, or while they sat on those high barstools (Gastón deduced that the bar must have been in the Large Dining Room of the Old House). And they were uncomfortable barstools that made you aware of the many hours of little work and those long spells in which not a single client would come in.

Finally, if one does come in, if he was one of the regular customers or had been given a recommendation and he's come to look for one girl in particular, then he'll ask for her. And if he's one of those who chooses what he wants on the spot, he'll go to the bar, order a drink, and pick one. But if he's one of those who is too embarrassed to choose, and there are many more of them out there than you can imagine, M. was explaining, there are even those who are too embarrassed to choose with all of them standing in front of him, so they use a picture album or a video, as if choosing one girl over another might reveal something more personal or intimate or less masculine (as if it's not real macho to decide on one woman over a bunch of others because, when all is said and done, a pussy is a pussy and, if he's a real man, one is as good as the other); hence, for those types the marketing director had imposed a rigorous system of taking turns and in that way everyone knew when it was going to be their turn, which leads to less arguing but it was no less boring. In reality, anywhere you go they always take turns, like where M. worked, but always, before taking the next client, the one who is up next would wait a few moments while the other girls went to war trying to force a decision and here, in this case, the brief opportunity for individual exhibition (they would also bet among themselves) had been eliminated by the practical and monotonous system imposed by the marketing director.

This explanation was very long and relatively unnecessary, since it only served to clarify why Claudia's friend Sandra who, in turn, had told this story to M., why precisely it was Sandra who was chosen to attend to that older man who was fat and poorly dressed and whose scrambling up the stairs of the Tajmahal (the Old House, Gastón remembered) had produced, despite the air conditioning, those enormous blotches of sweat on his light blue shirt that was out of fashion, and the drops running down his face.

It was an excessive explanation in terms of the purpose of this story and could be justified, Gastón analyzed, in terms of M.'s personal conflict with authority. Hence, he immediately created links between that marketing director whom M. didn't even know and her stepfather about whom she had spoken many times in their sessions.

But M. continued her story, despite everything, aiming toward what she thought were the most important parts (even though Gastón knew that wasn't true for, in reality, the most important in terms of his analysis of her were the excessive details about the marketing director that M. considered to be merely introductory details).

And amidst attentive daydreaming, M.'s words, and a piece of meat stuck between his teeth, Gastón listened, that is, he heard that during the summer the hottest hours of the afternoon were called "happy hours," because they gave substantial discounts to the clients and free drinks which explained why some fat guy would show up who didn't really fit the profile of the majority of the men who go to those places and while he grunted, Gastón, who was trying to dislodge the piece of meat from his teeth, heard that the fat guy hadn't shaved in two days and it looked like one of those white, prickly beards you see guys with in jail which was very distinct from the carefully unkempt look of the young lawyers who would trim their beards with a special tool. And while he was seeking triumph over the meat particle, Gastón, who because of his shyness was unable to assist his tongue in dislodging it with his fingernail, a shyness that he said to himself doesn't even make sense, given that M. was stretched out on the couch and couldn't see him unless she would raise up brusquely and turn at the same time. So, Gastón heard that the man was almost totally bald but seemed insistent on letting a few strands of hair on top of his head grow long so he could comb them to the back, making him look ridiculous and untidy, and Gastón finally raised his hand toward his mouth, controlling some of M.'s agitation, he wouldn't like her to see him when he, like now, put his hand to his mouth and fiercely fought with the nail of his index finger to remove the meaty fiber that was causing discomfort to his gums and then, Gastón, heard her say the man who was wearing old, baggy pants with safety pins, which were quite adequate for the fat guys with bulging hips, as in his case, who limped on his right leg at the same time he was observing everything going on around him; and not so much the women as the place, for his mouth fell open when he looked at the ceiling, and the walls, and he had bags under his eyes like President Alfonsín and when he began to talk he pronounced things strangely (he couldn't get that double rr to come out correctly) and then Gastón stopped listening, the buoy of his attention stopped floating and sank into the depths of deep attention because he began to suspect that what M. was narrating had something to do with him, something more than the fact that this story was taking place in the Tajmahal. Dr. Rimetka began to imagine that the man whose description he was being given so meticulously in the story must have been Uncle Pucho.

And when M. said that the man had paid to get in and instead of heading for the bar (which for Gastón, was undoubtedly the Large Dining Room) in order to take stock of the girls who were available, like all the men usually do, he turned around and went the other way, as if to see what there was near the staircase and he began walking, limping a bit, toward the administrator's office, at which point Gastón couldn't help but imagine Uncle Pucho walking through the Vestibule (M. was probably too young to use the word *Vestibule*) toward the Piano Room or perhaps the other way, toward what had been for so many years the bedroom where Gedalia, who believed in nothing, had slept in one bed and Granny, who didn't believe in anything either, slept in the other, all due to that curious, faithless religion that at times they prayed to but that prohibited them, for instance, from sleeping together in the same bed.

And I would like to know why the hell Gastón's patient told him all those details about something that didn't even concern her.

We'll never know what the patient told him or didn't tell him. The only thing we really know is the way Gastón told the story, one in which it was very probable he went about re-creating and combining details according to his own deductions, inferences, and suppositions that filled the logical voids, the few details that, in reality, his patient had told him.

Continuing, then, since Sandra's turn is next, she goes up behind the man and puts her hand on his shoulder and he turns about suddenly, smiling stupidly with a missing tooth.

Sandra takes a deep breath and hopes they'll finish quickly, that it'll be fast. Even though it's not that hot because of the air conditioning she still doesn't feel like working, Sandra, ah, those timid fat ones, she tells herself, they tend to get it off fast and in ten minutes you're back at the barstool or, in the worst case, supposing the guy wants to get what he pays for (they always think that way, they're going to stay there, resting calmly, but feeling uneasy and bored, then they get dressed and leave, they're all the same), and she'll be in the bed next to him, composed, smoking a cigarette with the satisfaction of having done her work correctly and judiciously. Sandra, acting especially pleasant, makes a simple comment about the summer heat so that the old man will relax (you're in a hurry, take it easy, Sandra says to herself, remembering that famous anecdote about Napoleon and his valet), she takes him to a room, but he says no, not there, that's the Middle Room, he tells her. Can't we go to the End Room? And Sandra doesn't understand until the guy explains to her that he wants a certain room and when she finally begins to get the picture, Sandra says no, they can't go there because she doesn't work in that room, that's Alexandra's room but, if need be, they can easily double the price and he can have both of the girls.

And so Sandra goes to look for Alexandra, and they like to work together, it's more fun, they enjoy signaling each other secretly from above or underneath him (it's that sense of bizarre humor that Alexandra has), but the man doesn't want to have anything to do with either of them, since he's already intimidated with just one of them. Now Sandra is getting so irritated with his insistence that finally she discusses it with Alexandra who lets them use her room, the one he insists on calling the End Room, even though now there's one more room at the end that was built over the patio.

So, what would you like to call me? And the guy stutters a name that Sandra, as she tells the story, can't remember now but seemed like a nickname, an ordinary name, anything, and she sees he's going to be one of those who makes her work for her pay, his armpits reek of Valet deodorant, he must have splashed Atkinson aftershave lotion on his face and neck, and he has that smell of an old man all over him, and now he's hugging her and shuts his eyes and says the name slowly and the poor guy can't get it up for anything, not even with a crane. Sandra thinks he must need a little romance and rejects her pat series of brutal exclamations (there are those who like to hear those impolite things, there's something for everyone on this earth), and she shifts into her romantic series, my love, honey, sweetie pie, and she was right, this is better, she knows her job, she congratulates herself because he manages to work up an erection, albeit flaccid and somewhat limp. Just in case (she wants to take advantage of all of her resources), Sandra offers to put on a video even though she anticipates his response, no, please, no movies, he embraces her again, and then presses his dick against her, it's not easy with that belly of his, she unfastens her bra, how annoying to have to let him enter slowly when you're in a hurry, wanting to finish the job quickly, but that's the way it goes, if she tries to hurry it up he'll be there the entire hour, it's better to shower him with sweet nothings, they come slowly, and the man lets out a prolonged, pitiful, restrained moaning sound, Sandra gets a little worried, is something hurting you, honey? My heart, the guy says, my heart hurts, he says, and instead of looking at Sandra, her eyes or her breasts, he's looking at the out-of-date picture in the frame, those little Hamilton girls (always a bit fuzzy due to the Vaseline on the lens) that the marketing director considered appropriate for decorating their rooms, and if I would've known, Sandra continues, if I would've realized, but no, like a foolish kid, come here, my love, my heart and soul, I'm going to kiss your heart like this, even though kissing his heart is not included in the price, Sandra, in order to get this over with, the guy is still dressed, this is incredible, and underneath his light blue shirt he's got an absurd undershirt, Sandra unzips his fly, she's only going to kiss his heart, in your birthday suit, and that's as far as little Sandra plays with the Disease, at least with a guy like that, who you can tell is about as promiscuous as a monk, this guy is more saintly than a saint, rarely are guys his age out doing the rounds, kiss his heart is the important thing now, Sandra calculates, so that his heart will perk up, become energized, red and pulsating, the minimum at least so we can get this over with, she says to him, my lips and my tongue have done their job quite efficiently, and now finally the rubber's on for protection, however you want to do it, she's about to ask but she's intuitive, she's discrete, that's why she's doing so well there, and has so many regular clients (and one other guy who doesn't go to the Tajmahal, the guy who is going to get her to pose for some ads for jeans, and thanks to those ads we're going to get the most out of your little buns, her favorite client says to her, the guy she practically doesn't charge anymore), our little Sandra is so sensitive, she comes to realize the best thing to do is not ask him anything, don't ruin the ambiance because it could end up that way and I'll have to start over from scratch, it would be a crime with the rubber in place and everything, what a disaster, so she pulls him down on top of her, missionary style, and begins to move her hips, assisting him, and the guy moans quietly, as if he was almost there, and it's true he was just about to come, Sandra will say, no lying, he was just about to . . . and then the S.O.B. has a heart attack right then and there. His face was pale, almost blue, then there was a cry of real pain, and now it really doesn't matter whether he's lost that fragile stiff dick because the scene has turned into something a lot worse, she tries to get up, screaming for help, call an ambulance. The Tajmahal will pay for it like it always does, this is not the first commotion (which is what they tend to call those cardiac arrests) they've had, but certainly the most serious.

However, they know it didn't happen that way, at least not with the logic of the way it was told and certainly not as detailed in the version M. gave to Gastón, which wasn't even her story and was of little interest to him. She had told it to him in a session in sketchy fashion as a prelude—a trampoline—to another story about her own personal anguish. And who cares about anguish or whatever motivates M.'s anguish, not us, that's for sure, not Gastón, who has remained silent while he tries to tie the fragments together into something that makes sense.

A fragment here and, due to its color and size, another there, which coincides with certain prior information, and finally it all begins to take shape for Gastón: clearly, then, the ambulance that left the parking lot at the Tajmahal with Sandra's poor, old, sweating, fat man, who had suffered a heart attack, is the very same ambulance that took Uncle Pucho to Saint Eusebius Clinic where Gastón had been visiting him, first in the Intensive Care Unit and afterward, when he was better, in a triple room that The Indian Girl made cheerier with flowers, a portable television set, a huge box of glazed chestnuts (that was mainly filled with paper) for her Daddy when they took him out of therapy. He hid them in a drawer and there was another (smaller but heavier) box of regular bonbons for the visitors.

Uncle Silvester said if it was Gastón who had talked about this, he did two things wrong: he talked too much about his uncle and he betrayed his commitment to professional secrecy. But he also said it's hard to know if it was Gastón because every man is innocent until proven guilty.

Aunt Judith said Gastón is so full of shit his eyes are brown. But she wasn't mad about it.

Gastón said he didn't say a thing to anybody.

Aunt Clara said her son would never, ever talk about his patients, despite her repeated efforts to get information out of him because these women's lives are more interesting than the soap operas.

Gastón said if rumors got started it was because people at Saint Eusebius Clinic, who got the information from the ambulance driver, told The Indian Girl.

The Indian Girl said the ambulance driver told her they found Uncle Pucho lying in the street, surrounded by a bunch of people, and that some doctor had called for an ambulance from a corner bar.

Aunt Judith was on the verge of saying it was nothing new or even worth going around gossiping about poor Pucho who couldn't get it up, for there must be some reason why The-One-Who-Isn't-Mentioned was on the rag and you should have seen his second wife's sour face when she was still well. But she didn't say anything because she cared a lot about The Indian Girl, who was her favorite niece and reminded her at times of her daughter Lilian with all that long, black hair.

The Book of Memories mentions in a trifling way that Uncle Pucho had a heart attack in the Old House. But not precisely in the Tajmahal, that is to say, not in the Old House when it was a massage parlor but in the Old House when it was a club for retired people, the place they called "I Want to Dance, and You?" that came long after the Tajmahal had closed down, when everyone had become used to democracy, and the men realized that the famous massage parlors offered the same thing as any flea-ridden flophouse and they continued going, of course, but only to the ones located downtown, that is, the ones near their work, and all that remained on the outskirts and other neighborhoods were apartments for call girls.

Pucho's heart attack in "I Want to Dance, and You?" happened on a Saturday night at exactly 11:50. It was before the dancing started but after they had drunk a toast. And Clara and Silvester were with him.

And this time the ambulance company didn't want to take him because by the time they arrived he was already dead and it was a real problem for his brother and sister and "I Want," first to get the police to come and then a hearse to take away the body. Because when you've got a dead body on your hands, everyone disappears.

This doesn't mean the story about what happened in the Tajmahal is false. It doesn't mean it's true, either.

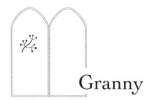

Granny

But can you really say something important in this language? Can you really say things you believe, say what comes from deep inside you, from your gut? Are there words for those things in Spanish? Spanish, bah. What kind of language is this? If you're hungry, you can say it: I'm hungry. If you want to do number two, turn up the television set, say this food needs salt, how much do you earn a month, take care of your daughter, she's crying, that's OK. You're right, you can say those things in Spanish.

But if want to say stop, don't bang on the tea kettle anymore, there you have it, a simple thing, nothing important, but it's impossible. If I tell you not to bang on the tea kettle in Spanish, no one is going to understand me, it's as if you're babbling nonsense. Then along comes my son Silvester and says to me in Spanish don't bug me, don't be a pain, and other things. But it's not the same thing. Everything is similar but not in this case. Don't bang on the teapot, how can I explain it to you? It's like a soup that has a different flavor to it, and another color, as if you added fried onions to it. Is food without onions going to taste the same as food with it? It's not the same.

Can a woman really tell a man in Spanish that she loves him? It can't be done.

That's the good part about being in this place, you can talk to the whole wide world. Almost everyone here speaks something. And the cold doesn't bother me that much. For the ones who were born here, perhaps, but those who never lived in Poland, or didn't die in Poland, let them gripe. You have no idea what it was like to dig in the ground that was hard as rock, and frozen, in order to bury someone in the winter. First you had to dig through the snow and then chip away at the ground that was like a rock. That was what you called cold. It's never like that here. Well, if someone wants to complain, you can find something to complain about, but not me, who had a life like mine and knew hunger like I did. Once, back in Lithuania, when I was little, they were washing me up to put me into a coffin, but the cold water woke me up. I had fainted out of hunger. In Poland. In Europe. Back there.

I don't suffer from hunger anymore. I don't have any problems either. The only thing is if you see my children I'd like them to change that picture of the monument. I don't know why they chose that picture when I'm so old. Who'd be interested in looking at that face. When I was with all of you, on that side, it had been a long time since I had looked at myself in the mirror, it hadn't been since I got that old, ugly face. And here I put it on every day.

Once they took a pretty picture that I'm sure Clara has. They didn't take it with color film because they didn't have it back then, but they painted the colors on, like in the old days, and all the boys and the women were blonds. But I was naturally blond and they painted my hair the color it really was and made my mouth red and you didn't see any wrinkles anywhere on my face. So for Hanukkah and Purim, which are happy celebrations, they would let us make up our faces like in the photos. During the rest of the year we have to go around with faces looking like we were on our death beds and I don't even want to talk about mine. When all is said and done, there must be some advantage to dying young. To think in my lifetime I never enjoyed myself and never cared about anything and, if it's because of my husband, religion was only mentioned during sad times and, here, I've got to force myself to celebrate. Even though I still don't care about much, you know what it's like: wherever you are, it's always best to do what the others do.

I know, I know, you're all alike, you want to know what it's like on this side. You think it's going to be so different. Here, there, what does it matter. It's all the same. And that's just fine too. Those who lived as long I did aren't going to get frightened when they find out that death is never ending.

And, yes, there's another favor I'd like to ask, now that you're going to talk to Clara about that picture: don't have them put Gedalia with me like they do other couples. It's no big deal, it's all the same, I put up with him there, I can put up with him there, so it doesn't matter. I say no for his sake, since we have so little space here, with two of us together we wouldn't be able to turn around. It's more for him because he dreams at night and then he tosses and turns and pulls the covers away. Here, whenever someone dreams, it's during the day. At night we're up and around. Basically, I never used to dream. What's the use, anyway?

So what are you, some kind of journalist? I know you who you are: you're Silvester's oldest son, the one who directs a boring TV program that we always watched, mainly because you're part of the family.

And do you think with that piece of equipment you're going to put us on TV? Don't you know that those of us who have gone to the other side don't appear in pictures? We don't show up in black and white, like they used to make the old pictures, much less in color.

And you can make your machine run faster or slower in order to hear us speak, but it will be the same as hearing nothing. You think you are the first one to think of it, smart guy, others already have and nothing works. Not just anybody can see or hear us: there's only a few who can. You should feel fortunate you are one of them, be lucky you're one of the rare people who can talk to us. It's not that I want to appear on television, although it's true I wouldn't mind the wife of the doorman and some neighbors seeing me, the ones who are still on that side. It's always nice to appear on TV.

Sure, that was quite an invention, that TV: the most important thing in the world for children and old people. Before, we had the radio which was also great. That's one thing I do appreciate in life: for a woman who had lots of work to do when I was a young woman, the radio was the best thing to come along because you could listen and have your hands free to do other things. Later on in life, when I didn't have as much work to do, there was TV and I could sit down and watch while I crocheted since my hands did it automatically, with a quick glance once in a while to change stitches during the commercials.

You want me to remember and tell you about it. You're crazy in the head. Why try to remember everything? I do what I have to at the moment: I don't look back, I don't look forward. And there's nothing to look forward to anyway. What I can see are my children, and my grandchildren, and I hope they are good at least for throwing dust over our eyes, for whatever there is to see. I've heard they throw dust over our eyes so that we won't envy the living, but it's probably better to say so that we don't suffer seeing the stupid things they do.

Sometimes I think about stupid things, like what kind of boys and girls I would have had with another husband. That's when you've got too much time on your hands. Granny stories, they're all stupid. My daughter Clara turned out well, my other daughter Judith turned out more or less. I loved the two of them equally: a mother is a mother.

A mother loves her children the way children will never love their mother. But Judith was always jealous, yes, was she ever jealous. Was it my fault Clara was such a good girl? A daughter is never the same as a mother. A mother sacrifices herself, a daughter doesn't.

All siblings are jealous of each other. When Judith was born, Pucho came down with a false case, truly false, of croup. I say that because the little girl who died of diphtheria had real false croup: the earth took a jewel away from me. See how stupid it is to try to remember. Is there really so much good in the world that it's worth remembering? Talk about the past? Rummage through your heart? Poor Pucho made strange noises with that false, really false croup. He couldn't exhale, so he'd turn red, then blue. Yes, I know he's around here, but they put him somewhere else, in a new area, and sometimes he comes to visit but not much. A son isn't a mother. And ever since he suffered that attack when Judith was born, that's when it all began, and Pucho became an asthmatic.

Oh, he was such a difficult child, and I worried so much every time I heard him breathe like that. And we went to different doctors, they didn't know how to cure him but they sure knew how to charge us for it. Learning how to soak their patients must be the first thing they learn in medical school, and I wish Silvester had become a doctor but it doesn't matter, he still got an important position.

One day, when I was still on the other side, I see Clara's son coming with two children of his own, says Granny, aren't you happy, my wife's pregnant. He thinks I should be happy about it? I don't know why. Just because the poor woman already has two to take care of and now she has three? Aren't there enough children in this world? Why more? Well, young people will be young people. *Young* is a word that goes with happiness. Even on that ship coming over, there was someone who sang and danced and that's what being young is all about. But I only threw up. On the ship there was this young boy, he was really educated and he played a violin. He wasn't Lithuanian, he was from Warsaw, and he'd just stare at me. When I started feeling a little better, we talked. And what happened to him? What did he end up doing? Nothing, he wasn't anything, he didn't amount to much, the poor bum. He became a music teacher. His name was Berel.

I was coming over because my fiancé Gedalia had sent for me. He had paid for the trip. He was more than a fiancé, he was my husband, according to our religion, even though we hadn't been able to get married lawfully back there, in Lithuania, because he had been an army deserter. I was a young girl at the time, but I had gained some experience in life and I also knew that it was dangerous for a young girl to talk to just any man because in Argentina there was the Zwi Migdal organization that deceived so many woman from Poland. They ended up in, what're they called? Brothels? But I couldn't have even thought anything like that about Berel, because he was not like those men that my mother and other women had warned me about. He was such a well-educated young guy, not a stupid butcher, he was someone you could talk to. He was with the rest of the men on the ship, on the third level, piled on top of each other, and the women had cabins. But we would run into each other, not necessarily at dinner time because I could barely eat, I would just throw up afterward, so we would go somewhere else and talk. The ship was large and those of us on the third level had to stay on that level. The doors were locked and they had people guarding the doors who wouldn't even let us take a look, but it was different for those on the first and second levels: they came down whenever they wanted and would look around where we were staying since they had purchased tickets that allowed them to move about the ship. Berel and I talked about our families that we had left behind and what we wanted to do in America. We just wanted to get jobs. It's not fair he died so young, a young man of fifty.

It's something I'm never going to understand: why do you people think we know everything? Whatever we don't know, we don't know.

And we'll never know either. For instance, just because I'm dead now why would I know what Pucho did with the money he took from his father's business during the time of those postdated checks. I didn't know before, I don't know now. The only thing I can say is that Pucho was a good son, but he was never very smart. If you want to know what I think, it wasn't a game at all for him, he never bet on anything, he didn't even play around with women, and there are a lot of them around for a young guy to pick up without having to spend a red cent. And don't forget he was married to Martita at the time, so he didn't even look at other women. If you want to know what I think, he wanted his independence, he didn't want to work with his father anymore, which is understandable, and he took from one business to put it into another, and he just dug himself a hole, deeper and deeper. That's what happened.

Look what good that money did: it was like putting a mustard plaster on a dead person, it was useless. And he really paid for his foolish life. Judith would always say that he was my favorite, as if a mother can love one of her children more than another. A mother can't do that, because a mother is a mother. Another thing, he was in my bed a lot when he was small, that's true, but you have to understand what it was like when he would have one of those asthma attacks: he'd become desperate because he couldn't breathe, it even got to the point that he would bang his head against the wall, so don't tell me that his getting into my bed wasn't justified.

You were asking me who was president when Judith was born. How do I know? Do I care who the president was? Like last year's snowstorm: what do I care? Are those important things in life? Here was the important thing in life back then: when I would breast-feed Judith I'd listen to "The Adventures of Carlos Norton," starring Roberto Salinas and Emma Bernal, on the Stentor radio station. It was a mixture of love and crime—now that was real life.

Gedalia always liked to listen to the news. Stupid things, Granny stories. Here are today's events, there are tomorrow's. Who cares. On the news casts today, when there is someone who is involved in a real drama, and you see that they're really suffering, then it's worth paying attention to. The only problem is that you want everything to turn out OK and the next day they've already forgotten about that person. And then there'll be another one crying and suffering and you never find out how anything ends.

But it's different and better with the soap operas, and I'll tell you why: they're based on stories that happen to people everywhere and all the time.

I couldn't imagine Carlos Norton with Roberto Salinas's face— he was the actor with the voice on the soap opera on the radio— and I had seen his face in magazines like Sintonía and others. I imagined him with Berel's face, the kid on the ship. Stupidities: what would Berel have to do with crimes and killings and the police? He was well educated and the only thing he liked to do was play his violin. He had sad eyes.

So, that's all I miss here, nothing else, just the soap operas on TV. But that's OK, and if there aren't any, there aren't any, so what. But we'd happier if there were. Everyone would be. You're mistaken if you think I'm the only one who misses watching TV. But I don't miss sad eyes. Sometimes a woman can see that a man has sad eyes because of something he ate and it upsets his stomach. Gedalia, for example, always had sad eyes whenever he ate lousy food at a restaurant. A woman has to respect her husband, if anything, for her children and for herself. I don't see why nowadays young girls have to get married so early. They're so young and they don't know what having responsibilities means. They're not aware that a husband means work.

That's what Judith and I would talk about sometimes, and Gedalia didn't know about it. Well, he suspected something, but he really didn't know. On the other hand, I knew fully well what was going on and we had good, long talks about it. I used to tell her don't be in such a hurry. Why hurry and what difference does it make when it's all the same anyway? This man or that man. So what? In the end he'll be your husband and it doesn't matter who you end up with because you'll still have to wash his clothes, add salt to his food, and make sure it's hot. You're going to create a dickens of a problem if you marry this guy, and he won't be any different from the rest: he'll always be just a husband. The important part is your well-being and that's all. A husband who knows how to earn a lot of money is better than a husband who doesn't. That's all there is to it. A husband who doesn't earn money is worthless and the rest is nonsense. There's no getting around it.

When I used to remember Berel's sad eyes, at times I would imagine him in the kitchen drinking liquid Vaseline in order to make his body move. Still, he didn't have to die so young, that I know.

Judith put up such a fuss over that Ramón guy and to what end? What did she get out of it? Spending her life laughing at his jokes, always the same jokes. I never understood them. There's only one thing that can make a difference in a woman's life, and it's not whether she marries this guy or that guy: the difference is to be independent. If only I could have had that little store I dreamed of. That was my big hope, and illusion, my dream was to become independent. I wanted to have a place on that same street, Rivadavia, and once there was a store for rent on a little street nearby. Even without a store, if Gedalia would have only given me a little money to begin, to set up shop in the hallway, even when times were not so good. Thread, buttons, ribbons, pins, elastic, thimbles, gimp, lace, bead and ribbon embroidery, all those little things. Not everyone had those things to sell, you have to be meticulous and well organized, and I could have been but I wasn't able to. I didn't even pay the servant or buy the underwear (whenever it didn't come straight from the cooperative) or when Judith brought home that Pelusita brand, so we even went together to buy underwear, and Gedalia was the one who was always in charge of the money.

But I'm talking about things that don't interest me; I wanted a husband and I had one, enough! And you have to respect your husband. Now then, I fought hard so that my daughters could become independent, study, and make something of their lives. But what was the use, nothing came of it.

And if not, then they should marry someone with ambition like Gedalia, a man who knows how to earn his place in life, which is why we came to America. He was not like that Berel guy whom I didn't see much after that and then when I did see him once I already had a fur coat that Gedalia had bought me, which was when he started to spend money, mainly to show off, you know, to make people jealous, and we also had a car. Berel dressed poorly with an old hat, some half-yellowed shirts which looked like the same ones he had brought over from Poland. Music teacher, bah! It isn't even a man's job, a man has to have ambition, he has to fight to make it in life. A skinny kid at twenty years of age is all right, but when he's thirty he needs to have a little fat around those bones. And at forty he should have a paunch that you can pat and a watch with a chain like they used to have back then. And the poor boy died at fifty-four, so young, it's just not right.

Here, the schedule is very strict and you have to comply with it: you sleep during the day and we get up at night, but you have to stay where they put you, with your neighbors, you can't go running around all over the place. That's why it's so important to have the right neighbors. But you still have to go around with the same face you had when it was your turn to go, only for Hanukkah and Purim do we get dolled up like in the pictures.

Sometimes, even though they have the best of intentions, your children don't think about those little details and they put you next to someone you don't even know and you end up not liking them or, what's even worse, they put you next to someone they thought was your best friend throughout life, when in truth you probably couldn't stand that person and, afterward, it's the same here as well. Perhaps that's what you thought about her all through life: I hope you're like an onion with your head stuck in the earth. And you never thought that your head was going to be buried right next to hers.

But, in the end, it's all the same. Since there are no TVs or soap operas here, I'd like to have my knitting needles and wool like they gave a lady nearby. Of course, I never knitted very well, the grandchildren always complained about it. Judith's daughter whined about having to wear sweaters that I had knitted, the ones in which one sleeve was always longer than the other and they'd have to fold them under the shoulders, which made them look like they had shoulder pads at a time when they didn't use them. The important thing was for the sweater to be warm in the winter time and made with good thick wool. And since it was also a kind of hobby, maybe here I could even learn to knit better. Frankly, I was a lot better at crocheting and everything in my house sat on small crocheted doilies that I had done myself and once I crocheted a sweater that came out a lot nicer than those other knitted sweaters.

Well, look at the one who's asking me the questions, oh, this one's a real joker: he thinks just because I'm dead I'm going to tell the whole truth and nothing but the truth. Not even those who died four hundred years ago tell the truth, no one does. But I can tell you something that is true: at one point I saw Berel quite often because he was teaching violin to some children in the neighborhood and he would walk by our house more or less at the same time, so I would step out and we'd say hello to each other or we'd talk for a few minutes, but I never dared to think about having coffee with him.

Frankly, I knew all about him, not because we always said hello to each other and that's all, but I knew about him from what others used to tell me, ship brothers, or different people who knew both of us because, in reality, there were a lot of us from Poland but there weren't a lot of us either. They told me he had joined a union, frankly I don't know which one would accept a music teacher, and he'd go to political rallies and play this and that on his violin for the workers.

Jewish workers, bah! Everyone is called a worker. At first everyone must have been a Jewish worker, even like me, because when I came I was a hemstitcher in a seamstress shop; others worked for tailors and some in larger factories. But after a few years had passed, there weren't any more Jewish workers, Jews are too clever to remain just workers, they have ambition. That's what they say about Israel as if it were a big deal, but I don't see it, they're all Jewish and they say that the woman who cleans your house is also Jewish, the factory workers are Jewish, the beggars in the streets are Jewish, the one who washes your socks is Jewish, the one who begs for money is Jewish. But I doubt if a Jewish woman is going to clean your house for very long. Even if she cleans it for several years, for sure her daughter will go to the university. It's the same with politics, I wasn't interested. If someone is going to be poor, they're going to be poor; who ever dies from hunger is destined to die from hunger—with or without politics. Luck: that's what you gotta have in life. The rest is unimportant.

Later I heard that Berel moved away to some small town near Salta and he married a store owner's daughter. But the store owner had many daughters. Which is to say he didn't inherit the store. And he was never anything more than a music teacher, a violin teacher, at a time when many people were losing interest in the violin. Berel, the poor guy, had no ambition, no nothing.

Similarly, I used to think about him when I watched soap operas on TV, especially the one sponsored by Palmolive at tea time, with María Aurelia Bisutti, Menchú Quesada, and Fernando Heredia, who was, yes sir, quite a man. The kids were all grown up by then, just Pucho, his wife, and his daughter lived with us. She was the second wife, the one who thought she was the great Krazavitzke. We were some of the first people to get a TV in this country because we brought one back with us when we went to the United States with Gedalia.

All of his brothers and sisters had them, so we brought one back and bubble gum for the grandchildren. Gedalia received an inheritance from his father who died in an old folks home. Here, in Argentina, he would have died in his own house but, up there, where everything is made of nylon and plastic, the old man died alone like a dog with fleas in a place they didn't call a home for the aged or caring center because they didn't use those words back then, but it was a place for old people.

So we bought it with the money from the inheritance, and because we were able to bring it back without having to pay taxes, we also brought a set of dishes for Clara who was already married, and I wanted so much to bring a set for Judith but I had to pretend she didn't exist, because of Gedalia. And the grandchildren got the bubble gum and caramel candies that you don't find here, and a large refrigerator for Silvester. And the TV was for us and Pucho, since he still lived at home.

Anyway, we came back on a ship with those things—the gifts— we had purchased and we arrived during a general strike by dock workers who belonged to some union, I don't remember which. That was the era when the workers would go on strike in order to defend that Long-tailed Devil. Oh, did Silvester ever give us problems with Perón! And we had bad luck, that's why I say luck is just about everything, nothing else matters, and we were unlucky because the freight containers with our things inside were hanging by a hook on a large crane. A worker left the crane unattended, the crane, that is, with our things hanging in the air, and he lets go of the winch and everything comes crashing down to the ground. How did it turn out? Half of Clara's dishes were broken, the door to Silvester's refrigerator was twisted, and the rest of it had to be repaired. We turned on our TV, the one that belonged Pucho and us, and the sound was perfect, but all we could see was a bright, narrow band across the screen which, in itself, was something to see. So we'd sit down to drink our maté, look at that thin strip, and listen as if the sound were coming from a large radio, because by that time small radios were more in style.

At first all you saw were those little tiny radios, the ones that were like a little tube, all the kids would crowd around together and try to listen to it all at once; later they got bigger, and during the war we listened to those big, loud radios, but then they got smaller again. I sure would like to have one now, even if it were one of those really cheap models but I guess I'd much rather have one of the big ones, which was the best era ever for radios, when I could listen to the Quintrala, Pérez García, and the programs that were worth listening to. And the news about the war, thankfully neither Gedalia nor I had left any family there, everyone had come over, and even here no one felt totally safe from the military because they didn't know if they were pro-Hitler or not. But, myself, I think they were.

And even now I say the same thing I used to say to Judith: a man can seem like glittering gold or one of King Solomon's largest jewels when, that is, he's far away. But when he's your husband, he's your husband, and that's it. And then what? Judith would have preferred I leave her father, her brothers, and her for another man? Why leave one man for another? They're all the same, nothing changes. It's not worth it.

And you think if I look deep inside my heart and dig way down and pull out what I really feel, because now I can see you, I'll say I wish I had married Berel instead of Gedalia? As if there were any difference! And I also see you haven't learned a thing. Because what I really wanted to do was sell notions. Berel or any other type of Berel didn't mean a thing to me next to what I really wanted, which was to sell notions, to be independent.

All I'm saying is why did he have to die so young? It wasn't fair for him to die at fifty-four, it wasn't right for him to die so young and me so old.

That's why I ask you again to talk to Clara and take care of the matter of the photograph, so I can fix my face for Hanukkah and Purim, for once in a year. Look here, I only have this one opportunity, and I don't want that picture of the old lady. Is that supposed to be me, that old thing, am I really a grandmother? Me? A granny?

Many Years Later

Aunt Clara said Martita, on one of her trips back to Buenos Aires, had called Silvester.

Aunt Judith said Aunt Clara couldn't have possibly known that because Silvester wouldn't have told anyone even if they had cut him up, not his wife, into little pieces.

Aunt Clara said she found out through Fortunée.

The Book of Memories states that in time and due to habit, Clara ended up befriending Fortunée, Silvester's wife, and stopped calling her The Dumb Turk. But not Judith.

Aunt Judith said she would've been the last person to find out.

Aunt Clara said Aunt Judith underestimated people and The Dumb Turk, I mean to say Fortunée, had found out about that phone call and many more because she always lifted the receiver in her bedroom whenever Silvester answered the phone in the living room.

She had to be dumb, Aunt Judith said, she was The Dumb Turk.

And she lamented the lack of intimacy in which he, her beloved brother, had to live during all those years. To have given away his pistol is one thing, Aunt Judith used to say, but Silvester had much better offers from women with more money and class.

And even though he knew it was a lie, for he was lying to himself, Silvester felt he had been waiting for that moment—that phone call—that reunion, for more than thirty-five years.

But since no one mentioned it, and there aren't any witnesses and it's not written down or documented anywhere, we're forced to wonder about what Silvester might have felt or thought.

With the passing of time, some faces get wrinkled and others grow flabby. And there are faces that get wrinkled and go flabby simultaneously which is even worse. Those creases and deep furrows that form around the eyes and cause young blonds to go into fits of desperation aren't really so dangerous because they don't change the shape of the face. On the other hand, there are facial changes that distinguish an old face from a young face: the loss of muscular tone, drooping eyelids, bags under the eyes, the shape of the face becomes spongy, less defined, then there's the double chin (or, with skinny people, the bulging craw), spilling downward in folds under the chin; sunken cheeks that used to be firm and now hang flabbily along the lines where people express themselves, flowing out beyond the outline of the face, forming two slight but bland protuberances, almost like two additional small chins on each side of the principal chin, which now fights to stand out from the others and show how it's different, or provide some form of identification in the middle of defused lines of demarcation. These are the signs that identify an old face which can produce such extremes as to erase any idea of the features that originally gave the young face an outline. Perhaps for these reasons it's difficult to see partial resemblances or, moreover, indisputable differences between young adults—each one a distinct owner of its own, singular face—and babies who look like other babies and old people who look like other old people.

In some part of his conscience, Silvester knows it's a lie, he hasn't been thinking about her for more than thirty-five years. He knows perfectly well that his image of the woman had disappeared from his mind—even from his dreams—a long time ago. And when she began to come back, she never caused any pain, pleasure, intensity, or grief that ever indicated she was important to him. In any event, the memory of that face reappeared among many others, but only from time to time, just before he would fall asleep; it was like a sedative, that is, like a supple, seductive, pliable memory, amid so many sheep ready to jump the fence of insomnia.

And it's only been during the last few years that he began to remember her as a real person, above all, over the past few years when he'd look at himself in the mirror and see the destruction, the horror that time has done to his own face, then he would remember her (and others as well who, for different reasons, he hasn't seen again) and try to remember the place where each wrinkle might be on that face, the contour of her droopy eyes, wrinkled and baggy eyelids, like a turtle, with that expression of devastation, resignation, or anguish with which each one of those faces must have confronted time (as if there were some way to confront it). But he thought more and more about her face. And, when he did think about her, he tried to be a realist and adapt the shapes of her face, the ones he remembered arbitrarily, like the circumvolutions of an ear, a certain way of looking out the corner of her eye, the triangular intensity of her chin (because memory is impure and nonsensical), and adapt them to the possible reality of the moment when they are remembered: he tried to pull, soften, and wrinkle that face, comparing and superposing it to others through which he had been able to substantiate the devastations that time had wrought.

Silvester used to tell his children that people are like trees: they are born, they grow, they produce fruit, and, when the fruit is ripe, they're done, they've completed their mission in life.

He said that with rational conviction, using the same energy with which he asserted that religion is the opiate of the people and all the social laws that were imposed by Perón had already been proposed by Alfredo Palacios long before.

Sometimes his children would get distressed because they thought they were already mature and independent, a fruit that had ripened or, in fact, they were now full-grown trees bursting with their own fruit, new fruit, not yet ripened, and they didn't like the idea that their father should feel like he's already fulfilled his destiny and has no further use on earth.

But Silvester didn't feel that way. As always, even though he attempted with lucid energy to adapt his emotions to the pigeonholes that his mind assigned to each one, Silvester would always fail. And so he looked for a rational justification that would permit him to respect his feelings without modifying his theories. How can a tree really know when its fruit is ripe, when, although not all, or not every one of them, have already fallen from the branches? And now he was referring, of course, to that other tree that included its trunk and roots, the factory that had flourished and distributed its products in stores throughout the city. The factory that he, personally, had built up while his father-in-law spent his time on multiple and diverse but always fleeting business deals that he was particularly good at and had the necessary mental agility to get into and out of the same businesses that always flopped on those who got into them too late (like Pucho), or too soon (like Pucho), or didn't know how to get out of them (like Pucho). The factory that he finally inherited from The Ottoman, that is, the factory that his wife had inherited and, hence, had brought them together more than love or affection or even just living together, that business which brought them together forever and in indissoluble fashion, and where one of his children worked with him, side by side, Silvester imagined, and even though his son doesn't agree in any way with this supposition, even though his son doesn't feel at all as an equal but clearly subordinate to him (and it would be interesting to compare his feelings with Silvester's who, in the factory, sees himself as the trunk and roots of the operation); and even if his son were in a distinct position in the factory, it would be so much better (and that should be said with objectivity) than the place Silvester and Pucho had in Grandfather Gedalia's business.

And it should also be said objectively, even though it's not written down anywhere, much less in The Book of Memories (where there are no intimate feelings or thoughts by anyone) that Silvester, when he was headed for that strange, unexpected appointment, he wasn't thinking so much about her face but rather his own.

Because, like a good seducer, he was less concerned about what she was going to be like than what the reaction on his face was going to be and the impact he was going to have on her. Once a good seducer, Silvester hoped he was still a good seducer or at least able to please an ugly woman or a dumb one or, for whatever reason, one who wasn't very attractive, even an old woman.

And, in his life as seducer, not only had his principles not collided with his actions but also, to the contrary, the fact that he had been a free thinker and, what's more, a Trotskyite at one point in his youth, permitted him to stand at ease and once in a while whisper his seductive discourse (but also in a way to himself and in a normal voice with an alert conscience, ready to judge and condemn) in terms of the concept of free love that he preached and practiced whenever the opportunity presented itself.

Thus, whenever it was necessary, Silvester persuaded the women he not only desired but also loved, albeit briefly, to believe that feelings of love deserved to be consummated above and beyond social laws and conventions. And they accepted and felt solidarity with that fabulous idea about freedom but only because it was wrapped up in the idea of its opposite, the idea of love, that implied some type of confinement, being chained up, stuck in prison, and so they openly practiced with Silvester that absurd contradiction called free love, at the amusement park or in the old houses of ill repute, in some run-down motel, in apartment-hotels, and afterward, even though less frequently, in some transitory lodging, the free love that Silvester practiced so well without clarification, because he didn't think it was necessary, that as well as free it was also brief, although that didn't mean it wasn't sincere or intense, it was love that lasted exactly the amount of time Silvester needed to love, in terms of the other more brutal meanings that one tends to give to the verb, to those women who almost immediately, one after the other, suddenly find themselves, freely, with something in common: they had ceased to be loved.

And in another era, when it wasn't necessary to become deeply involved in intellectual or philosophical discussions in order to take a woman to bed and make her participate in defying the norms established by an unjust society (which is always disposed to go against the demands of nature), in the marvelous challenge of what is known as free love, and it wasn't necessary simply because the norms had changed and physical relations between two people were more acceptable and permissible, and no one talked about free love anymore or even hardly remembered what that strange expression had meant at one time, even though Silvester still continued talking about love to those women, but without the need to use the adjective *free,* in those places that were later called dives, temporary rooms, and apartments, and in some swimming pool along the Pan-American Highway. And the women continued to be caught by surprise (because despite all those social changes not one of them, not even the younger ones, had changed so much that they weren't seduced by the word *love* that still carried concepts of prison and the like) due to the ephemeral nature of the love that they had proposed and consummated, and then consumed by it.

And if one were to think of some reason, beyond family reasons, that would justify why Silvester, through the years, would always think of Martita in particular and perhaps with feelings of anguish, it's important to keep in mind the many characteristics of that relationship that had made her distinct from all the others; for example, like the particular and anguishing fear that in Martita's case the word *love* had produced in Silvester, perhaps because in that one singular case it hadn't worked for him, the idea to associate love with the word *free*; for example, the deep and happy friendship they had during many of their childhood and adolescent years; for example, the unabashed fact that never again, except for some vague comment by her cousins, Martita's twin cousins, never again did Silvester hear from her, because ever since her divorce from him and escape with Sam Sim, Martita had never attempted in any way to communicate with anyone in the Rimetka family, by mail, telephone, or in person, during her trips back to Argentina which she must have taken to visit her family.

And that's why, thanks to the uninterrupted perfection of her absence, similar to being dead, his memory of her was absolute and untarnished, Martita, wearing her dark blue suit, missing one sleeve, in addition to those stripes, and her green eyes and her enchanting way of getting everyone to follow her around or have others lead her around, or perhaps both ways simultaneously, dragged or pulled, and in different ways, she takes what seems to be immobile, rigid, and impossible, and puts it into motion.

Due to all that, Martita's return or perhaps one of her many returns or, better yet, that particular time when Martita decided to call Silvester on the phone and after rejecting different bars and coffee shops that didn't exist anymore, because through the years the city had been undergoing change, or (worse yet) they were still there but they were different, altered, not just old but converted into something distinct, or (worse yet because there are always worse possibilities) it was a place that was still there but had been slightly altered in some way, creating a type of caricature of itself by having added marble and varnished wood and spirals and boisseries and awnings; after discarding all of those places for diverse painful reasons, they agreed to meet in the old but still dignified Ideal Coffee Shop in order to talk like two mature adults who have memories to share, in the accompaniment of the pianist Osvaldo Norton, none of which is written down in any part, or appears in detail or at all (except, perhaps, there's a picture) in The Book of Memories, not because it's more recent, memories are recorded constantly and each event and each voice is a memory as soon as the sound dies out, but because there are no witnesses who are capable of superimposing their memories until they juxtapose certain elements allowing their memories to come together, to amass, to condense in those darker, coincidental, indisputable regions that, finally, become the ones that acquire that risky honor of becoming part of The Book.

It's important, then, for those who know his personality and his life, to recognize the high probability of being able to conjecture successfully about Silvester's conscience.

It's important, then, to recognize the startle he received upon hearing that unexpected voice that he instantly recognized on the other end of the line, but to which he showed professional indifference and provided a neutral voice with which he spoke from that moment on in order not to alert Fortunée, who as always was listening to his phone call from the bedroom, and he, maintaining the tone of a business meeting until he realized and even admitted against his own free will that he was talking to a woman who was old enough, although it wasn't revealed by her voice, not to cause concern for the woman who had decided to live with him and their children and, above all, with his free and ephemeral loves (that she knew all about), although in spite of that reason still became uneasy each time she began to suspect that a new, beautiful butterfly was dancing briefly around the somewhat less intense but nevertheless lighted flame of her husband.

It's important, although there's no document to prove it, that in reviewing and reconstructing the Rimetka family history while Silvester was walking on a Thursday afternoon in what used to be called downtown and is now called the Minicenter, reviewing and reconstructing their history that he wouldn't want to alter or falsify in any way, but searching for certain events that he could tell Martita with some happiness or with dignified sadness or, at least with farcical grace, the parts of their history that Martita could possibly find interesting, above all, the people with whom they had been around, which eliminates the latest generation of Rimetkas about whom Silvester had much to say but not necessarily to her.

We have to accept that Silvester thought about not mentioning Grandfather Gedalia who, ever since the sale of the Old House, sat permanently in a covered chair in the modest downstairs floor where he had lived with Pucho and continued living with Pucho's daughter and her husband, all sitting alone at the small table that they had salvaged from the house, wearing an old pair of dirty, wrinkled pajamas in that small, old, dirty, run-down apartment, with all of his old strength dedicated to making sure the door to the patio remained shut because of drafts of the cold air. Grandfather Gedalia, after his Collapse and then, above all, after the operation on his hip in which they had replaced the top of the femur with a platinum screw, could only walk if he held onto the back of a chair that he would push along the floor ahead of himself. And for that reason he almost always preferred to sit alone at the small table with a glass of water in which his own phlegm floated on top, gently swaying back and forth every time

Grandfather Gedalia would touch the table with his hands or his knees, bursting against the light into thousands of little white or yellow opaque streaks, without mixing with the water. Even though Daddy Gedalia was still lucid enough to make decisions and to sign documents, he was unable to keep his foreign accounts a secret, the same ones about which no one knew hardly anything as long as Daddy Gedalia was capable of inching his way to the mail box and about which everyone found out afterward even though it was impossible to convince him, Grandfather Gedalia, now weak, thin, and deaf, but absolutely lucid, that one of his children should appear next to his name as holder of those bank accounts whose growing contents he always feared would disappear due to the irresponsibility or dishonesty of the younger ones, those children of his who were already grandfathers themselves but who, according to Daddy Gedalia, were always considered the boys.

Silvester won't tell Martita about Granny's death or about the horrible state of senility which she had suffered during her last days, frenetically crocheting little tablecloths with her hallucinating needle and thread, working day and night, without eating or sleeping, her poor hands. She was now unable to dedicate the attention necessary to her most basic necessities because she couldn't stop, not for one instant, crocheting that magical, invisible tablecloth whose interruption, she believed in her state of delirium, would have brought on disaster and catastrophe, a cloth that her conviction and the precision of her movements transformed at certain moments into something so real that you could almost touch and admire it.

And while she was crocheting, Granny would talk about Pucho and his business and the postdated checks and the cloth store and digging a hole deeper and deeper for himself. Anyone would've realized that she wasn't talking about crocheting but about the money she had amassed with her husband (even though she never had the opportunity to spend it the way she wanted to use it or, simply, to count it), in sufficient amounts in order to live without constraints during many years but never in sufficient amounts (because no amount would've ever been enough) in order to be able to live without having to worry about it.

On the other hand, Silvester would also tell Martita, most likely, about Clara and they would laugh together (but in a friendly way) about her doubts and being overweight and the special way about her, having no opinion of her own, he would tell her, for instance, how Clara would see things through her father's eyes, through her husband's eyes and, finally, to speak through her son, and Martita would probably get upset at him (but in a friendly way) for making fun of his sister and she would ask about Judith and he would give a big sigh and begin to tell her the sad story of Judith's life, who had suffered so much, but who was so strong, quick to respond, foul-mouthed, quarrelsome, and always defiant, capable of scandalizing her own children, not so much Pochoclo as poor Lilian, who had been a tough militant of the Peronist Left Wing (but what would Martita, after so many years abroad, know about this monster of late, the delirious, dissipated, and agonizing Peronist Left Wing), she was so severe, poor Lilian, while she was alive, and so much more responsible than her mother.

And, at last, Silvester would talk about himself, just about himself, his success in industry, the importance of his factory, the only business of its type in the entire country, a money-making, efficient operation, capable of adapting the fluctuating economic cycles that affect the economy of the country, capable of becoming a spore during lean times and then flower during the brief but intense periods of the good times. And it gave Silvester certain pleasure to rediscover the successes to which he could make reference: the good life, a mature tree bursting with fruit. And, most likely, neither one of them would talk about his other brother if it wasn't pertinent.

On that Thursday afternoon at 5:15 P.M., Silvester went into the Ideal Coffee Shop. Everything was just the way it was supposed to be: the marble tiles were in place, the columns were there, the piano music was just right, and the pastries were lined up with their honey coating shining through the glass cases. But there was that low-intensity, ugly, horrible, horrible light (which he hadn't expected) coming from those fluorescent tubes.

And he barely sat down when Martita arrived. Silvester had been worried that the devastation caused by time would have hidden her real self to the point of making her unrecognizable, someone else. But as soon as she walked in, he knew it was she: wearing pants that before would have simply been tight but now were too tight; wearing high heels that were just a little too high, and a blouse with a slightly low neck, the colors of which were a tad too loud and only slightly out of place. And, hence, half closing her eyes to create that out-of-focus look, her vision barely veiled by the liquid sheen over her eyes, her appearance could have been perfect—Martita as always, audacious Martita, sporting that almost savage elegance so normal for young people, only that she wasn't young anymore and if you looked closely you would see she was an old woman, who had dyed her hair bluish black, a woman who looked like a foreigner and she had the expensive, ugly shoes to prove it, a woman who dressed like a tourist but without that exaggerated or clumsy look, not like a young woman dressing up for Carnaval (sporting a camera and a violently flowered shirt), but like the characterization by an intelligent actor directed by a sensitive set designer.

And her face wasn't flabby or wrinkled but firm, slightly rigid, with that stereotypical partial smile and lifeless eyes. It was a face from which an artist (a surgeon who is also an artist or, at least, a very competent craftsman) has erased the more evident signs of old age without, however, going back to her original condition that he probably couldn't have known except in pictures, that is, frozen in a superficial pose that had become a part of an ignored, forgotten movement that the camera was unable to capture, which is wherein lies truth and grace. It was a face that immediately revealed Martita, without a doubt;

it was like recognizing with certain horror the original face of which a good caricature was making fun.

And then Martita began surveying the tables and the people who were there, but she didn't recognize him.

Silvester wanted to get up and leave; instinctively, he raised his hand and waved to her.

And then it was all verve. Of course the verve was still there. And the happiness. But now it was forced. Only now did Silvester realize that Martita always talked too much, she had always talked a little more than he wanted to listen to, but never before had he given this characteristic sufficient importance to be able to define it, never before had he even thought about or remembered it; now, however, Martita was talking and talking.

She talked about her life in California, about the homosexuals in San Francisco, her children and her grandchildren, the man who was president of her adopted country where, for sometime now, she has been a citizen (and that man is, in another country, an open topic among people with a certain cultural background), and she talked about human rights and, in particular, women's rights, her work, and her retirement, about her husband's success as a musician in Hollywood (that despite his lack of international prestige he was important in the USA). And Martita talked some more and took pictures out of her purse, trying to void the present by calling up far-away images, filling the spaces dedicated to words, involuntarily highlighting the horror—the pounding sounds of silence—in which they could have found themselves.

If he had wanted to, if he had accepted the cards he was dealt and played out his hand according to the rules she was trying to impose, Silvester could have talked about politics and economics too. Martita was sufficiently knowledgeable so that she could participate in a long conversation in which they could compare the evolution of North American foreign trade with the situation concerning the balance of trade at the present time in Argentina. Or Silvester could also talk about the Rimetka family just as he had planned on doing, and maybe even more, if only he had accepted the rules of the game, if he had been strong enough.

But, instead of taking the easy way out, saying what was expected of him, Silvester looked into Martita's eyes—those eyes that were still green but without the green fire that once upon a time had stoked feelings of desire—and asked her if she still remembered the Japanese Park.

Silvester had made a reference to an incident that could have been insignificant and unimportant but, at the time, became important for them; in fact, it was critical and produced an impact on them; it was an event they had talked about afterward and could remember together, one that had occurred so long ago it seemed inconceivable that even as far back as then they could still have a past even more remote to remember together. Silvester, who had stopped smoking, worked with nervous hands to convert the paper napkins of the Ideal into serpents, little canes, and elongated forms of his pain. He was also unable to explain why he, feeling so much anguish, needed to know they were able to share that memory.

The Japanese Garden, Martita said, where we would buy food to feed the goldfish.

No, said Silvester, it wasn't the Japanese Garden he was thinking of, but rather that other place in Retiro Train Station. The Japanese Park had also been Retiro Park, back when the station was almost new, run by the English, and it was clean. The Japanese Park, with the Shooting Gallery, the Tunnel of Love, the House of Mirrors, and the Fun House. Do you remember, Martita, Silvester said, while she looked at him without looking at him, lifeless, without those bags under her eyes, expressionless, you mean to say you don't remember the Fun House, with the moving floor and the chair that would fall apart and the blast of air that lifted the girls dresses while the guys below watched. Don't tell me you can't remember, Martita, Silvester repeated, even if you don't remember anything else, don't tell me you can't remember the Fun House.

And Martita said yes, in Disneyland. . . . but how was he to know if she really remembered or not (and is it possible she could have forgotten, covered over, or denied a part of her life like that?). Precisely because she remembered so well, because she knew it would be important to him for them to be able to share that memory, that's precisely why she played it down, pretended to remember only vaguely, giving it little importance, or, if she really didn't remember at all and just said yes, of course, in order to avoid a situation that was boring her, or wanted to change the subject. But, either way, Martita was lying. And the second possibility was just that much more painful, that is, her indifference, and having to suffer ever so sweetly the pain of revenge from insult, instead of having to put up with forgiveness or, worse yet, the monster of being completely forgotten.

Before leaving the Ideal Coffee Shop, Martita gave Silvester a picture in which she and her husband were surrounded by their children and their grandchildren in a lusciously green yard with no fences and a large white house in the distance, flanked by other green yards. That's the picture in The Book of Memories and the only proof that the two actually met each other.

And Silvester believed the S.O.B. was already making payments come due in this life. And he was referring, of course, to the pact he hadn't wanted to agree upon when the Devil (who didn't smell of sulphur or have a trident but who was definitely Satan) appeared before him, simply because he wasn't disposed to believing in the Devil or accepting his existence.

But even without the pact, which was still unsigned, the Devil had afforded him his gifts and, since Silvester who was a free thinker and ex-Trokskyite, wasn't able to accept the idea of another life after death, the Devil was making payments come due in this life.

Because, for those who don't believe in the afterlife, old age is living hell.

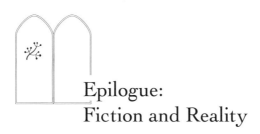

Epilogue:
Fiction and Reality

"Grandfather crossed through the mud in Tomachevo, but he really wanted to cross the ocean. So he went to the consulate of this poor America where, he was told, they didn't pay much attention, they didn't understand anything, it was all the same to them. That's America too, but not quite. What's important is to leave Europe, to be able to cross the ocean. Then it'll be easy to get from one America to the other America.

They didn't pay much attention, or they didn't care, or they didn't understand anything, and so Grandfather got ready to cross the ocean. Grandfather Gedalia Rimetka—always elegantly dressed but a little too skinny—boarded the ship in Odessa and started the crossing.

The ocean was wide, the ship was Italian. The men slept down in the hold. In the bilge? Grandfather Gedalia didn't know the word *bilge*. Everyone vomited but him. Gedalia, tall and skinny, watched his fellow travelers vomit everywhere. There were Polish and Russian travelers on board, and Italians who had gotten on in Genoa. They ate a lot of pasta on board the ship. Lots of macaroni and potato dumplings, but no ravioli. Round pasta, flat pasta, Bologna-style fettuccine with meat sauce, or pesto. That's why by the time Grandfather reached America he wasn't skinny anymore. He gained forty pounds in twenty days. Grandfather ate a lot of pasta but he never got sick. After they reached Brazil, he also ate a lot of bananas.

They arrived first to Pernambuco, where there were many blacks and Indians, and it was hot. Grandfather didn't like it there. This is America? his fellow travelers asked, feeling deceived. Give up that mud for this mud? Doesn't look promising. Hot mud here instead of the cold mud in Poland? But they loaded up with bananas. And that's how a young, skinny, adventurous kid left Odessa and how a dour, fat Grandfather Gedalia arrived in Buenos Aires. He always refused to eat strawberries. "They're everywhere in the forests. Bananas are another matter."

This text that I wrote several years ago, at a time when I didn't know that it was going to become part of the first chapter of my novel (although I had hopes), could very well be a warm and precise evocation of my own grandfather: my Zeide. But it is not. This is fiction: a combination of memories of known grandfathers and imagined ones. There are memories that I would give back to their real owners. I have no idea where the others came from; for instance, I don't know anybody who might have boarded a ship in Odessa, much less an Italian ship.

After writing this first text (that at the time was left sadly to its own), I became interested in comparing fiction and reality and I decided to conduct some research on the ship (that is, on the ships) in which my grandparents had come to Argentina. After putting a small notebook in my purse to write down information, I called my Uncle Mauricio, now eighty-five years old, who is a nephew of my deceased

Grandfather Musa, both of whom had come from Beirut. I had my Grandfather Musa and my Zeide Meishe, and it took me many years to realize that both of them were called Moises.

The Schoua* family in Beirut was middle class. And if one generation of the family used names like Musa, Mojluf, Sebulum, Sara, and Rebecca, the younger members used French names—Maurice, Richard, Adele, and Jacqueline.

My father's sister, Aunt Rachel, married her cousin Mauricio. My Aunt Rachel Schoua invites me to eat *mamules,* an Arab pastry, while Uncle Mauricio is determined to make it perfectly clear that he didn't come as an immigrant.

How is that? I ask him. Did you come as a tourist, by chance? Uncle Mauricio is worried I'm going to confuse the different social classes or mix them up, so he wants to make sure I understand that the Schoua family from Lebanon, who are cultured, middle-class people, are higher up on the social scale than those on my mother's side, the Szmulewicz family from Poland, who are poor and ignorant.

He didn't come over like my Polish grandparents, who came by the thousands piled up in the bilges of those ships. He traveled in second class on an English steamer that departed from Cherbourg. And he chose second class because he couldn't stand having to wear a tuxedo for dinner every night. More than anything else in the world, my Uncle Mauricio is worried I'll confuse Beirut at the beginning of the century with a "steitl" in Poland, and he couldn't find the words to describe how beautiful and modern Beirut was. He left because he wanted to, because he was adventuresome: he took a Messagerie Française steamer to Marseille, then he went on to Paris, and from there, to Cherbourg. His people spoke Arabic and French, not Yiddish and Polish like the others.

* My real name is Ana María Schoua.

His memories of the trip are pleasant: good food, dancing every night, but he feared that all of America might be like Pernambuco, and, of course, those amazing bananas. And don't think for a minute, Uncle Mauricio insists, that we didn't have bananas in Beirut. But they were more expensive. My uncle got off in Rio de Janeiro in order to visit some Syrian-Lebanese friends who were living on Rua Alfonsega. And on December 5, 1924, when it was hot and humid, he arrived in Buenos Aires.

My grandfather was waiting for him at the dock to take him to the large Schoua family home in Flores, where I was born and from which I had to remove all that Arab furniture with mother-of-pearl inlay in order to install, in my novel, a very Polish family, the Rimetkas. That house is probably the only true character in the novel that didn't suffer some kind of transformation, except for those changes triggered by the arbitrary nature of memory. At some point in Argentine history the house was really converted into a massage parlor (a euphemism for brothel), which was called the Flores Parthenon.

Uncle Mauricio's memories after he got off that ship are ones that he shares with my aunt. But shared memories never coincide. When Uncle Mauricio and Aunt Rachel begin to argue about the differences in their memories, I get up and call my maternal grandfather and tell him I'm stopping by to visit.

Since you're coming anyway, why don't you bring me four pounds of fish and I'll trade it with you for some chopped liver. Fish is expensive, liver is cheap: my grandfather is eighty-six years old and he still tries to make deals.

I find them sitting in the dark in order to save electricity. My Grandmother, my Bubbe isn't interested in remembering anything and, after so many years of marriage, she has become respectful and silent. Let him tell you about it, he's the one with the good memory, she says, I don't remember anything.

But it's true they didn't arrive together, so I insist each one tell me their own story. My Zeide's memory is escaping him but he makes up for it by inventing stories. One thing certain is that within a year of each other, they both departed from Cherbourg, having traveled from Poland on a train. My grandfather was from Derechin and my grandmother was from Varsovia. Both of them remember the smell of freshly baked bread in a small hotel in Cherbourg where they probably both stayed.

The trip was cheap, Grandmother says. It cost $35, Grandfather states with such precision and certainty that his statements become suspicious.

I departed in 1922, says my Zeide. The ship, which was called the *Uruguay*, was English. I remember it perfectly. Whenever my Grandfather tells a lie, he scratches his nose.

I don't remember anything, Bubbe says. I stayed in a cabin with a woman who got off in Brazil. I was seventeen years old and seasick and I couldn't hardly eat anything and I vomited all the time. The ship was Italian and served lots of pasta, but I only ate fish.

Crazy musings, Grandfather says. What do you mean you stayed in a cabin? We were in third class, all piled one on top of another, packed in like sardines.

Yes, the men were, the men were all together, but the women had cabins, Bubbe says. I was traveling with my cousin, but he was with the men.

There were 1,800 passengers on board, my Zeide says. Numbers always gave him a feeling of security. There were Poles, Yugoslavs, and Germans. They treated us badly. We didn't bathe for twenty-one days. We stopped in Lisbon, Ecuador, Brazil, and Montevideo. I got off the ship at every port.

All of us brought something we could sell, my Grandmother said, mostly religious things because we knew that in Buenos Aires they didn't make those things yet. I took a . . . you know, to put on your head. And others took . . . to wrap around your arm. Bubbe is old now, she can't remember the words, she doesn't even remember them in Yiddish. It's been so many years since they stopped practicing or even talking about religion. My Zeide doesn't believe in God. My Bubbe doesn't believe in God either and, besides, she's not on speaking terms with him.

Whatever it was you brought with you, was it a talit by chance? I asked her. Yes! That's it! she answers. And how come you know that name? And she asks me with the same surprise when she found out I was attending a meeting of Jewish writers. And do you think you are a Jewish writer? What kind of Jewish writer writes in Spanish? But she had brought a talit and managed to sell it right away. What luck! They didn't let us get off at any port, states my Grandfather. They had us holed up like cattle. I remind him with some cruelty that he had just said they got off at every port. Well, yes, we did, he said, thinking quickly. He has lost his memory but not his intelligence. I was different, I knew German, they let me work in the kitchen and we'd get off the ship, go into town, and buy food.

They brought the food out to the ship in little boats, Bubbe says. In Portugal there were small boats that surrounded our ship bringing grapes and, in Brazil, bananas. And there were the religious types who couldn't eat anything, just bread, cheese, sardines, olives, and fruit.

My Grandfather remembering the boats and the hunger, takes a deep breath. Happiness? Sadness? Our lives were like radishes, he says. Like *jrein*, you mean hot radish, because of its taste? No! he says angrily. It was bitter, bad, sour, so much misery. But he also remembers a proverb in Yiddish: for the worm inside the radish, even radishes seem sweet. They were really poor. But they were also very young. To be young was almost better than having dollars.

What did you dream America would be like? I asked my Grandmother. She is a hard person, she has had a hard life. There were no dreams, she says, there was only work and making money, getting a position in life: that was our only dream.

I left them arguing about their memories of the immigrant hotel and I returned home to begin writing the first version of this text. And, then, sitting in front of the typewriter (I didn't have a computer back then), I suddenly realized this story has no end to it because my Zeide and my Bubbe had two children, each one of whom had two children of their own. And, between 1976 and 1977, the year the military junta took over in Argentina, the four granddaughters, including myself, boarded a ship of immigrants. While my sister and two cousins, the latter of whom were in a hurry, boarded a plane, I crossed the ocean on an Italian ship called *Eugenio* C. The ocean was wide, the ship was Italian. And we ate a lot of pasta. There were many Jews who were children and grandchildren of Russians or Arabs or Poles, and there were many Gentile children and grandchildren of Italians, Yugoslavians, and Spaniards. And we were all undesirable South Americans, *sudacas.* My objective was France but most of the others got off in Spain. And, thus, Spain, thinking it had gotten rid of its Jews, began to receive this new onslaught of Argentines with strange names that ended in -berg, -vich, or -sky.

And if all the Jews who arrived in the Americas were tailors, all their grandchildren who returned to Europe from Argentina were, by some strange genetic mutation, psychoanalysts.

Of the four cousins, I'm the only one who returned to Argentina. I love my country, and I educate my children to love our land and also to be aware that no matter how great this love may be, not one of us can be assured we won't once again some day have to board a ship of immigrants. I pay tribute to the ship that brought my Polish grandparents to Argentina, and the one that brought my Lebanese grandfather here as well. I pay tribute to the airplane that took my sister to the United States of America and to the ships in which my children and the children of my children, wandering once again, may well depart in the future. I pay tribute to my Argentine heart and my contradictions, I pay tribute to maintaining our Jewish identity in the Diaspora, To the ship of immigrants, this toast.

And I repeat the words of an old Sephardic song:

We lost Toledo,

We lost Zion:

There is no consolation.

DATE DUE

JUL 20 2000			

Demco, Inc. 38-293